At Home
in the Universe

At Home in the Universe

EXPLORING OUR SUPRASENSORY NATURE

Five Talks at The Hague
November 13–18, 1923

Rudolf Steiner

*Anthroposophic Press

This book is a translation of *Der übersinnliche Mensch, anthroposophisch erfaßt* (vol. 231 in the Collected Works), published by Rudolf Steiner Verlag, Dornach, Switzerland. The five lectures were given November 13–18, 1923 at The Hague. They were translated from the German by H. Collison and first published as *Supersensible Man* by Anthroposophic Press, New York, 1945. This edition was compared to the original German and revised by the publisher.

Introduction and Afterword copyright © 2000 Paul Margulies
Text copyright © 2000 Anthroposophic Press, Inc.

Published by Anthroposophic Press
3390 Route 9, Hudson, N.Y. 12534
www.anthropress.org

Library of Congress Cataloging-in-Publication Data
Steiner, Rudolf, 1861–1925.
   [Übersinnliche Mensch, anthroposophisch erfasst. English]
At home in the universe : exploring our suprasensory nature : five talks at
The Hague, November 13–18, 1923 / Rudolf Steiner.
   p. cm.
"Translated from the German by H. Collison" — T.p. verso.
Includes bibliographical references (p.).
ISBN 0-88010-473-2 (pbk.)
   1. Anthroposophy.   I. Title

BP595.S894 U2513 2000
299'.935--dc21   99-088286

10 9 8 7 6 5 4 3 2 1

Printed in the United States of America

Contents

Introduction

Paul Margulies

1. Background

The Earth is not our home. Our true home is in the world of stars. The Earth is our school. What we learn during life on Earth prepares us for our life at home in the universe. We look up at the stars and are stirred by their majesty. But without some sense of our suprasensory nature there is an overtone of sadness in this experience. Without some sense that we are spiritual beings we feel neither at home in the world of stars or here on Earth.

> Over the centuries it has become very natural to teach our school children that a newer worldview demonstrates that the Earth is merely a "speck of dust" in the cosmos, and that this speck of dust, together with an even smaller speck of dust—the human being—moves through the universe with delirious rapidity. It is said that this human being is completely insignificant in relation to the grand cosmos. This notion of Earth as a speck of dust has permeated every human mind and heart, and as a result people have completely lost the ability to connect humankind with what exists beyond the earthly realm (page 20).

This is the opening statement for these lectures, given in The Hague during November, 1923. They are essentially an intimate and deeply esoteric description of our journey through the planetary spheres and the world of stars between incarnations. Rudolf Steiner covered this theme many times, always from a different point of view. It was first presented in his book *Theosophy* (1904) and again in *An Outline of Esoteric Science* (1910). He gave many lectures on this subject as he toured Europe during the years 1912 and 1913, as if in preparation for the impending tragedy of World War I. In The Hague, he returns to this theme, but this time more from the inner experience of an initiate. Steiner's lectures toward the end of his life (he died March 30, 1925) present more difficulties for the reader than his earlier lectures. The approach seems to be more from within, trying to describe what it actually felt like to be speaking out of the developed consciousness of an initiate, and attempting to distinguish between the three higher states of consciousness, *imagination, inspiration, and intuition* (See afterword).

We experience the journey as states of initiate consciousness, as deep insights into our "humanness," and as the marvel of our transformation from the moral spheres of the cosmos into the muscles and bones of our physical bodies. There is an underlying tone of urgency: please understand; recognize what it is to be human; it is important. These lectures can be seen as a prelude to Steiner's last great lecturing activity, the lectures on karma and reincarnation in 1924, collected in the eight volumes of the series titled *Karmic Relationships*.[1] November 1923, when these lectures were given, was almost one year after the devastating loss of the first Goetheanum, and one month before the decisive Christmas conference and the refounding of the General Anthroposophical Society.

New Year's Eve, 1922–1923, Dornach, Switzerland. The flames blazed forth into the night, shot through with the colors of oxidizing metals used in the construction of one of the most amazing

---

1. Rudolf Steiner, *Karmic Relationships*, 8 vols., a series of lectures given throughout Europe during 1924, Rudolf Steiner Press, London.

buildings ever seen on Earth. Through the labor and love of men and women from fourteen countries, the Goetheanum was constructed during the First World War, within the sound of battlefields where hatred raged. Ten years of spiritual energy, devotion, and sacrifice went into this building, destroyed by arson in one night. The Goetheanum, designed by Rudolf Steiner, was a visible expression of anthroposophy. Every detail, every inch of the great domed halls, the carved columns, the painted ceilings, expressed spiritual forms that kindled the spirit lying dormant in each human being. Now it was gone. Most of the people who watched it burn were people who had helped build it. Heinz Müller, a Waldorf School teacher from Hamburg, was one such witness:

> It burned for a long time before anyone was able to see flames from outside. When at last they worked their way out into the open—the lights were still burning in the auditorium—a few dared to climb the western staircase once more and, shielded by the organ loft, took a last look into this great hall.... We were called back, as the danger of collapse grew greater by the minute, and shortly afterwards the sparks leapt to all sides as the two cupolas crashed in. Soon the columns, reacting to the heat, began to bend slowly to both sides. They stood like glowing, radiant lilies in the scorching flames. Above the red glow to the west the entrance vestibule held firm. The entire western section, built of the hardest wood, was still intact, and as I climbed the slope up to the carpenter's shop I saw Rudolf Steiner pointing towards the west and say to those standing near him, "Impress this moment on your minds." As I turned around, I saw how the organ pipes were beginning to glow, coloring the flames green and blue. The terrible splendor of this color still rose as if in warning against the midnight sky, as the bells of the New Year sounded in the distance.[2]

---

2. Raab, Klingborg, & Fant, *Eloquent Concrete*, Rudolf Steiner Press, London, 1979, p. 32.

This tragic ruin reflected the state of the Anthroposophical Society at that time. For esoteric reasons, Rudolf Steiner had kept himself separate from the society. After the war, the society was in disarray, torn by dissenting factions and by many well-meaning but failed initiatives not sufficiently grounded in anthroposophy.

Instead of sinking into despair, the sixty-two-year-old Steiner reached down into unimaginable inner resources to rebuild the Goetheanum and to refound the General Anthroposophical Society at the Christmas conference of 1923, this time with his participation as general secretary. And so 1923 was a year of increased activity: nurturing the fledgling daughter movements (the Waldorf schools, the technical and pharmaceutical laboratories, the therapeutic work, the new artistic impulses in theater, speech, and eurythmy, the biodynamic farming, the movement for religious renewal), increased lecturing activity, designing the new Goetheanum, and founding a new form for the Anthroposophical Society.

Before the general society could come into being, each of the local societies had to be reestablished on a firmer basis. Steiner hoped they would become more open, less sectarian. The five lectures in this book were given in The Hague at the refounding of the Society in Holland. During those five days, Rudolf Steiner also visited a Waldorf school, and lectured to teachers, to physicians, and to the general public. The loss of the Goetheanum and the increased intensity of Steiner's activities had taken its toll. Dr. F. W. Zeylmans van Emmichoven, who was to become the general secretary of the society in Holland, recalls meeting Rudolf Steiner at the station:

> I went with a few friends to fetch Dr. Steiner from the station. As the train slowly came in I saw him sitting at the window. I was shocked by his pallor and utter fatigue—and at the same time I saw in his face the hallmark of eternity. It was as though the

countenance were chiselled out of rock—an impression that went through my very bones.[3]

The medical lectures took place in the newly founded clinic, a private house where the very young Dr. Zeylmans van Emmichoven worked with a nurse. Some thirty-five doctors and senior medical students gathered for the two lectures, which were "surprisingly well-received." Most of the audience were hearing about anthroposophy for the first time. At the end of the second lecture one of the older doctors addressed Rudolf Steiner:

> He said that the lectures made a great impression upon him, that they represented an integrated system in which, admittedly, there were many gaps, but he realized that these gaps would be closed in further lectures. "My natural-scientific worldview is also an integrated system," he added, "equally with gaps to be filled, but these, too, may disappear. For which system am I to decide?" The doctor who put this question was sitting in the very back. Dr. Steiner walked slowly through both parts of the room to him and said: "You are perfectly right. More cannot really be said. But it is the heart that makes the decision."
>
> The doctor telephoned me the next day and said that although he was not entirely convinced, he wanted to give anthroposophical therapy a "fair chance," and asked me to treat him for angina pectoris (*ibid.*).

Dr. Zeylmans van Emmichoven goes on to describe the meetings for the refounding of the society in Holland. For the most part, Dr. Steiner sat patiently waiting.

> What he wanted, of course, was that the members themselves should find what the situation required. While the talk was proceeding ... he took out of my hand the tobacco pouch which I

---

3. From "Rudolf Steiner: Reflections by Some of his Pupils," collected in the *Golden Blade*, London, 1958.

had inadvertently drawn from my pocket, scrutinized the zipper, then recently invented, and said to me: "What a pity that an anthroposophist did not invent something so ingenious" (*ibid.*).

In the first of the public lectures (as opposed to the lectures to members of the society contained in this book) Rudolf Steiner addressed the consequences of the idea of "limits to human knowledge," an idea that was (and still is) prevalent, growing out of Kant's philosophy. Kant held that we can know only our experience of things. Our experience is transmitted through the senses, and the senses have been proven to be unreliable. Therefore, we can describe our *experience*, the *phenomena*, but we can never know the *reality* behind the experience, the *noumena*. We may theorize about the reality behind our experience, as we do with atomic theory, but we can never *know* the reality. The realm of the *noumena*, ultimate reality, Kant left to *faith*. We cannot know reality. It is as if someone poured a bucket of ice water on our heads. As Steiner points out:

> [The doctrine of *limits to knowledge*] gives rise to an uncertainty that undermines people's whole inner life, even though they may deceive themselves about it. That is a fact everywhere apparent to those who observe our civilization without prejudice. Indeed, it is characteristic of our time that we deceive ourselves in just these deepest concerns. But they are nevertheless active below the surface of consciousness. That is where they take effect, not as theories, but in the whole mood of soul, in aspects of soul-confidence and vigor.
>
> That is the *inner tragedy* that can be observed today in the soul depths of even the most superficial individuals. It is the reason for the *longing* for supersensible knowledge that many people feel, a longing that may seem paradoxical to us in the present epoch. We might say on a spiritual level it affects us as *hunger and thirst*.
>
> If we can't sense our belonging to a spiritual nature and feel ourselves to be beings who take up spiritual forces and substances and

have them within us, there is no possibility of knowing ourselves to be spiritual human beings. But in that case we necessarily lack self-confidence about what we nevertheless feel to be our most precious and dignified characteristics, the very ones that make us human beings and strivers after humanness (PL I. p. 2).[4]

Echoing the ancient inscription over the oracle at Delphi, "Know thyself," Rudolf Steiner once described anthroposophy as "awareness of one's humanity." And in his last written work, which appeared in 1924 as "Letters to Members," he described anthroposophy as:

a path of knowledge (cognition), to guide the Spiritual in the human being to the Spiritual in the universe. It arises in man as a need of the heart, of the life of feeling; and it can be justified only inasmuch as it can satisfy this inner need. He alone can acknowledge Anthroposophy, who finds in it what he himself in his own inner life feels impelled to seek. Hence, only they can become anthroposophists who feel certain questions on the nature of man and the universe as an elemental need of life, just as one feels hunger and thirst.[5]

In the second lecture to the public, Steiner contrasts the detached, "shut-off and self-consuming" tendency of natural-scientific knowledge, which leads to egoism, with the health-bringing aspect of a knowledge that participates in the spirit, a knowledge that connects us "quite practically with the moral sphere." Rather than thinking of knowledge as "true or false," he would have us consider whether or not it is "healthy or unhealthy." Knowledge that includes the spiritual leads us to

4. Public lecture given in The Hague: "Anthroposophy as a Need of the Age," November 15, 1923, available in typescript under the title "The Transcendent Human Being."

5. Rudolf Steiner, *Anthroposophical Leading Thoughts*, p. 13.

examine our conduct as either moral or immoral. In earlier times, Steiner reminds us, human beings didn't use the words "true" and "false." For ancient humanity, knowledge was either "willed by the gods" or "not willed by the gods." The word *true* comes from the German *treu*, meaning "faithful." Something was either "faithful" to the divine order or "untrue" to it. This "healthy" aspect of anthroposophy is described by Friedrich Rittelmeyer, one of Steiner's pupils and a founder of the Christian Community. (This is the name given to the movement for religious renewal for which Steiner acted as adviser at the request of several theology students in 1922.) Rittelmeyer, a well-known Lutheran minister, explains how he first approached anthroposophy. He tried to be open to it, neither believing nor disbelieving, assuming that "it might be right." And he tried to test its effects in actual life.

> But then the health-giving effect of anthroposophy was quite unmistakable. For the first time one had the impression that here was the true relation between Spirit and Nature. One became "healthy" in the real sense, realizing for the first time the utter poverty of the unspiritual materialism which has even laid hold of Christianity. And one became really "man." For man can only live if he feels himself a citizen of two worlds. When he has a great "over-world" above him—a world of which he can become a member with his own particular tasks—then and only then does he become fully conscious of the dignity of manhood.[6]

2. Molten Metals and the Ancient Priestly Sacrifice

The five lectures that follow, describing our life after death, were given to members of the society. As such, they were familiar with the anthroposophic image of the human being and with the basic

6. Friedrich Rittelmeyer, *Rudolf Steiner Enters My Life*, Floris Books, Edinburgh, 1963, p. 86.

facts of our journey through the planetary spheres. For a more complete background to these themes, see the afterword. Lecture five of this book contains a remarkable description of the initiate's experience, through *inspiration*, of tracing the veins of metal coursing through Mother Earth, veins of copper, gold, silver, and lead, condensed out of the cosmic fires that brought our planet into existence.

> *Inspiration*, through which we look so deeply into our own inner being, assumes a particular nuance when we consider that what can be described as our experience in the life between death and rebirth also lives in us during our life here on Earth. Indeed, all the grandeur and cosmic majesty that must be portrayed by describing the true human being as a denizen of the starry worlds—and indeed even the worlds of the higher hierarchies—is also alive in us as we stand here on the Earth, seemingly insignificant creatures from the spatial perspective within the skin of our physical bodies. Inasmuch as our knowledge can penetrate what we contain as a physical heritage of our true being between death and a new birth, we can also do something more; we can penetrate to the depths of our planet Earth, to its veins of metal ores of lead, silver and copper, to everything that lives as the metallic elements of the rocky Earth (page 93).

For the initiate, these metallic veins contain cosmic memories that trace the Earth's evolution back to earlier states of existence, as it condensed from an original state of warmth into gas, then liquid, and, finally, mineral.[7] The activities of the highest hierarchies are revealed in these processes, the work of the seraphim, cherubim, and thrones.

---

7. In *An Outline of Esoteric Science*, these states are called Old Saturn, Old Sun, Old Moon, up to our present designation as Earth; see especially the chapter "Cosmic Evolution and the Human Being."

If we look at metal under the influence of intense heat, at a foundry, for example, we can get an impression of the "destiny" of a metal, and this can lead to an amazing insight into the human being. Steiner compares the human being to the animal. Acknowledging all the anatomical similarities, he asks us to recognize the significance of the fact that the animal's spine is parallel with the Earth as opposed to the human being who stands upright. In this vertical orientation to space "we see the marvelous forces that allow children also to find their bearings within the dynamics of the universe." And we follow the marvel of learning to walk with learning to speak and, finally, learning to think. And in contemplating this uniquely human development in all its sublime beauty, "we see with higher vision metals melting in the fire."

> The archetype of this power [enabling a child to stand upright] is revealed when flames take hold of the metal, making it flow. As the metal becomes more fluid, it becomes more volatile, and we have a clearer perception of the inner resemblance between that process—which is, in fact, metal's destiny—and the smelting and volatilizing process in cosmic fires that enable a little child to walk, speak, and think. (page 101)
>
> This kind of knowledge links earthly death with resurrection in our life beyond the threshold. Such knowledge reveals the kinship between the cosmic fires by which metals are melted and the powers that make us truly human; thus the whole world becomes one and we realize that our earthly life between birth and death is really no different than our life in the spiritual world beyond the threshold. Life between death and a new birth is a metamorphosis of earthly life (page 102).

Steiner urges us to consider this connection between metals melting in the fire and the child's miraculous ability to walk, speak, and think, to meditate upon it, to deepen our understanding. If we can take this image into our imagination and meditate on it, a force will strengthen our soul and help us pierce the riddle of karma.

We can come to a real understanding of human destiny and karma through the twofold experience of seeing a child learning to walk, talk, and think, on the one hand, and the melting and vaporizing of metals subjected to fire, on the other. Karma is revealed in the fiery smelting of metals and in the appropriate transformation of a child's animal nature into human nature while learning to walk, talk, and think (page 103).

We are intimately related to all the mysteries of the natural and spiritual universe.

The metals melt, majestic flames of the fire's forces flow out to the very limits of macrocosmic space ... they turn around when they have gone far enough out into the cosmos and return as the forces that lift a child into uprightness. What we see on the one hand, we find also on the other. This gives you a picture of the ascending and descending cosmic forces of metamorphosis and transformation that work in the spirit of the cosmos (page 104).

In this, we find an insight into the priestly sacrifice of ancient times. The offering to the gods arose heavenward in the sacrificial flame so that it would return as a blessing for human beings. It was accompanied by a prayer:

O flame, I commit to you what is mine on Earth. As the smoke ascends, may the gods accept it. May what is borne upward by flame become divine blessing, poured again upon the Earth as creative, fructifying power (page 104).

Did Rudolf Steiner have this in mind when, watching the Goetheanum rise in flames, he said to those around him, "Impress this on your minds?"

1. A Speck of Dust?

NOVEMBER, 13, 1923

MY DEAR FRIENDS, I am certain that you realize the great satisfaction it gives me to be with you again to talk with you about anthroposophic matters. Of course, this is seldom possible, but when it does happen we can establish a direction for further work on matters that concern us. And this is always the basis for our being together, even when we are unable to meet physically.

We are brought together this time to form the Dutch Anthroposophical Society. Given the present conditions, it is vital to establish the societies of various countries so that a truly individual foundation is established to meet adequately the needs of our time. The General Anthroposophical Society will be established at Christmas in Dornach, and it will come into being only when the individual societies of each nation are represented in a way that their delegates are truly able to express the essence of each anthroposophic entity. Thus, by establishing the General Anthroposophical Society, we can to do something that is very necessary, significant, and important. If you can share with me a sense of how vital these matters are for our time, we will all acquire the right mood for our days together. And it is in just such a mood that I express my own most cordial greetings and heartfelt gratitude for your kind words to me.

The theme proposed for our lectures is the suprasensory human being as it is perceived and understood through anthroposophy.

We will attempt to express suprasensory knowledge and understanding of the human being from many different perspectives. Since there can be only a few lectures, I will plunge right to the heart of the matter.

When we speak of ourselves as suprasensory beings, we are immediately at odds with the way the human being is described today. For quite some time now, no one, not even one of the idealists, has spoken about our suprasensory being. The conventional culture and knowledge of our time never mentions the being who passes through births and deaths. Over the centuries it has become very natural to teach our school children that a newer worldview demonstrates that the Earth is merely a "speck of dust" in the cosmos, and that this speck of dust, together with an even smaller speck of dust—the human being—moves through the universe with delirious rapidity. It is said that this human being is completely insignificant in relation to the grand cosmos. This notion of Earth as a speck of dust has permeated every human mind and heart, and as a result people have completely lost the ability to connect humankind with what exists beyond the earthly realm.

But there is something that speaks to us today, though it remains unconscious, and we are unaware of it. It speaks today in clear, unmistakable tones, and urges us to turn our attention once more to the suprasensory nature of our own being along with that of the world. For the past few centuries materialism has found its way into our very knowledge of the human being.

What is this materialism, really? Materialism is a worldview that sees the human being as a product of physical substances and forces. Although there are many who maintain that the human being is not made up only of physical substances and forces, we have no science that investigates the aspect of human nature that does not arise from earthly substances. Today, when well-intentioned people say that the eternal in human beings can be understood, nevertheless, such a claim is not completely honest.

It is not simply a matter of refuting materialism. Today it is thoroughly superficial to want simply to disprove it at every opportunity.

The most important thing is not the theories based on materialism, which create doubt about the spiritual realm or completely deny its existence—or at least the possibility of knowing that world. The important matter is the tremendous significance of materialism. Ultimately, what is the purpose when those motivated by some condition of soul or by religious traditions say that human thinking, feeling, and willing must exist independently of the brain—particularly since contemporary science comes along and removes parts of the brain bit by bit, primarily as it investigates the brain in pathological states, while at the same time seeming to dispose of the human soul a little at a time?

And what is the use of some soul disposition or religious tradition leading to talk about the soul's immortality if the only remedies we can think of to help someone with a sick soul is to administer remedies for the brain and nervous system? Materialism has produced all this. There are many who are prepared to disprove materialism today, but they really do not know what they are doing. They cannot appreciate the tremendous significance of the detailed knowledge materialism has given us, and they have no idea of its consequences for our whole understanding of humankind.

So, let us begin here. We will go right to work by looking at the human being honestly, just as modern science does, and thus something will then reveal itself to us. Using all that physiology, biology, chemistry, and other sciences can contribute to our understanding of the human being, we will learn how the various substances and forces of the Earth come together to build muscles, nervous system, circulatory system, and the various senses—in other words, the whole human being spoken of by conventional science. Here we encounter a striking body of information; we find modern science in its most successful manifestation.

Let us consider, for example, the knowledge that medical students must have concerning the human being as the basis for their work of healing. Having become acquainted with certain preparatory sciences, they then move on to subjects that are fundamental to medicine. Let us imagine that we are looking at a handbook that collects everything such a student is required to learn about the human being. Imagine, here is a summarized textbook of all that the doctor must learn about the human being up to the point of going into a specialization. Now let us ask ourselves what this is. What do we know about the human being? We must say that we know a great deal; we know all that *can* be known today. But when we turn to psychologists, whose vocation is to understand the soul, we encounter an atmosphere of doubt and uncertainty.

First we become aware that natural science has attained valid and worthy results through research. It is so good, in fact, that lecturers on science are often unequal to the task themselves. Students are extremely bored by what they must listen to in premedical courses. This is not because of natural science but those who explain it. We should never say that science is boring, only its professors. Indeed, the fault does not lie with science, because science certainly offers solid and beneficial material. I want to say that, no matter how godforsaken scientists have become, science itself is good. But when we turn from the achievements of genuine, scholarly research and listen to psychologists and philosophers speak of the soul or the eternal aspect of the human being, we quickly realize that, aside from what earlier traditions left us, it is all words—nothing but useless words. Today when we turn to psychology or philosophy because of the deepest needs of our soul, we are not merely bored but find nothing at all in answer to our questions. Consequently, we can say that only natural science offers real knowledge today for those who seek it.

What does natural science teach us about the human being? It tells about what comes into being as a human being at conception or birth and what passes away at the time of death, nothing else. In all honesty, we must admit that science has nothing else to offer. There is only one alternative for those who want to be honest in this area. They must turn to something that cannot be gained through today's conventional scientific methods—a true science of the soul and spirit based, just as ancient spiritual knowledge was, on *observation* and *experience* of the spirit.

Such a science can be attained only through the kind of methods shown in my books *How to Know Higher Worlds*, *An Outline of Esoteric Science*, and others. These methods enable us to truly perceive the spiritual and to speak of it just as we speak of phenomena in the physical sensory world, which has led to the development of a healthy natural science. The earthly object of our senses and research has not been exhausted by any means, though it is well on the way. But it yields only knowledge of the transient, material aspect of the human being living in time. Thus we can never see beyond the earthly realm as long as we try to understand the human being only through such natural scientific methods. When we look only at the earthly, we see only the transient aspects of humanity.

We will see, however, that this transient human aspect can not be understood in and of itself. We are challenged to turn from the Earth and look out into all that surrounds it. When conventional science does this, it merely determines distances to the stars, describes their courses, and examines their spectra, or light phenomena that tell us the stars contain substances like those found on Earth. This science of the realm beyond the Earth, in fact, does not go beyond Earth at all. It is powerless to do so. Therefore, to begin with, I want to speak to you of certain points that will be confirmed in the later lectures.

When we direct our gaze out to the world of stars rather than limiting our observation to Earth and modern science, we first encounter the planetary system of heavenly bodies, which in a certain sense are related to Earth. They move in a way that is believed to circle the Sun, similar to the way Earth moves around the Sun. The planets also move along with the Sun through cosmic space. One can gain such knowledge through observation and calculation, but it is not useful to us as human beings. This sort of observation really contributes nothing to our understanding of human beings.

Suprasensory sight leads us immediately to something else. We gaze toward the neighboring planets as they are situated beyond the Earth—Saturn, Jupiter, Mars, back to Earth itself, Mercury, Venus, and Moon. In this sense, we regard the Moon not merely as a satellite, but as a planet, like Earth. Contemporary science calculates that Saturn, for example, takes thirty years to move around the Sun in its immense orbit; Jupiter needs a much shorter time, and Mars even less.

Let us look out into the starry heavens at a star—that is, a planet at a particular point in the sky. Elsewhere, we see another planet—Saturn, Jupiter, and so on. We look with our sensory eyes and see Jupiter here or Saturn there, but they also have an *etheric sphere*. It is embedded in a fine, delicate, ethereal substance. When we look at Saturn, for example—an oddly formed planet appearing to ordinary sight as a sphere surrounded by rings—if we can perceive the ether as well, we see that it accomplishes something in the ether surrounding it.

Saturn is active in the ether that contains and encloses its planetary sphere as a whole. The eye of the spirit sees that Saturn radiates forces, which may be perceived as a *formation*. The physical aspect of Saturn is only one element of the picture, one that gradually fades before the eye of the spirit. A spiritual view gives us the feeling that the *world spirits* gave Saturn its position in the heavens for our benefit, so to speak, to show us the direction in which to look. When we look with a spiritual eye, it is as if something were drawn on a blackboard merely as point of reference and then something is drawn all around it, after which the point of reference is erased. This is what happens automatically for spiritual sight; Saturn is blotted out, but what surrounds it becomes increasingly clear and speaks a wonderful language. Once Saturn is blotted out and we see the form worked into the ether, then we find that this form extends all the way to Jupiter, where this process is repeated. Jupiter erases itself, and what manifests in the ether spreads very far, and again a formation arises in the ether. This combines with the form from Saturn to produce an image in the heavens.

The same thing happens in relation to Mars. Then we come to the Sun. Whereas the outer, physical Sun blinds and dazzles, we find that this is not true of the spiritual Sun. All the dazzling quickly dies away as we gaze at the spiritual Sun. A great, majestic, living picture arises from everything inscribed into the ether, a picture that extends to Mercury, Venus, and Moon. Thus, we have the image as a whole with its various parts.

At this point, you might suggest that there are times when Saturn, for example, comes to a place in the heavens where it does not connect with the image formed by Jupiter. Strangely enough, this is also accounted for, because what we see comes together in an odd way. If you make a line in the Earth that extends from a certain point in the East, or Asia, through the Earth's center, elongating it from the other side out into the universe, such a line would assume an extraordinary significance for our spiritual sight as a whole. If Saturn lies beyond this line, we must carry the picture that arises from Saturn over to the line; there it becomes fixed. These images always fix themselves for our view by means of this line. Wherever we may see the image of Jupiter or Saturn (and we must look for them), they are fixed in our sight by this line.

Now we have a completely unified picture; our planetary system presents a uniformly formed picture. Do you recognize this picture? Once we figure it out, we discover that it is a cosmic image of the human skin and our sensory organs. If you could draw an image of the cosmos from the human skin and the sensory organs, it would depict exactly what I have just described. The planetary system inscribes in the cosmic ether what exists in the human being (as specialized by earthly conditions) as the three-dimensional image of the skin's surface, including the sensory organs. This, then, is the first thing; we discover a relationship between the earthly human being (our form given by the skin that encloses us) and the planetary system that shapes and builds the archetypal, heavenly picture of the earthly human being into the ether.

Then we discover a second phenomenon. We see the planets in *movement*. If we look at a particular planet, the Ptolemaic and the Copernican systems each present a different image of the path it follows. This may very well be the case; pictures of planetary movements can be interpreted in the most varied ways. But more important, however, is the fact that we can perceive all these movements together.

Saturn has the longest distance to go and requires the longest time to complete its orbit. Its movement, in conjunction with the movement of Jupiter, gives us a picture. And if we look in this way, then a whole picture arises from the movements of all these planets taken together. And we can reinterpret the picture that arises from the movement of the planets. This picture does not agree with astronomical descriptions of the planetary movements. Strangely, spiritual sight does not find the ellipses found in astronomical maps. When, for example, we follow Saturn with spiritual sight, something is revealed that, seen in conjunction with other movements, forms a figure eight, or a kind of lemniscate. And all the other various planetary movements play into this, and this presents still another picture.

The picture that arises from all the planetary movements

reveals itself to us as the heavenly image of the human being expressed in the nerves and adjacent glands. Spiritual sight discovers this archetypal image of the human skin and sensory organs in the sequence and arrangement of the planets. We have seen what happens when we go from this to the image of the planetary movements. If we draw an outline of the human form, we may sense that this outline represents the *form* of the planetary system. But when we include the nervous system and the secreting glands, with every stroke we have the sense we are drawing a physical picture of the movements of the whole planetary system as seen by the eye of the spirit.

Now we can advance another step in our spiritual observation of the cosmos. We have reached the point where we have a picture of the planetary movements by including in our drawing the nerves and adjacent glands. Now we can progress in our knowledge. As we do, the various movements fade away. When we rise from *imagination* to *inspiration*, the individual movements vanish.[1] This is extraordinarily important. What one can call "seeing" in the narrower sense disappears from the whole picture; it is suddenly gone. Now, however, we begin to "hear" spiritually. What was movement before now becomes indistinct and vague, swimming into one another, until it becomes like a picture seen through a mist. Out of this misty image, however, the *music of the cosmos* begins to form; cosmic rhythms become spiritually audible to us.

Now we can ask, What must we add to our outline of the human form that corresponds with these cosmic rhythms? As we

---

1. Rudolf Steiner uses the terms *imagination, inspiration,* and *intuition* not in their usual sense, but to describe inner capacities that are attained as one ascends to higher levels of spiritual awakening; see, Rudolf Steiner's *Stages of Higher Knowledge* and "*Imagination*—Imagination; *Inspiration*—Self-Fulfillment; *Intuition*—Conscience" contained in *A Psychology of Body, Soul, & Spirit: Anthroposophy, Psychosophy, Pneumatosophy.*

know, through art all sorts of transformations are possible. As we outline the human being and, within that, the nervous system, we have the feeling that we have actually been drawing. Nevertheless, we cannot directly paint what we hear in the realm of cosmic music, because it is all rhythm and melody. To represent this in our picture, we must take a brush and, following the nervous system, quickly dab some red here, blue there, again red, and again blue, and so on along the lines of the nervous system. At certain places we feel a pull to stop. We must reach out and paint in a special "form" that expresses what we hear spiritually. We can indeed transform what we hear there into drawing, but when we want to place it within the outline, we must at certain points widen it to make a completely different structure, because here the rhythm blue-red, blue-red, blue-red suddenly becomes melody. We must paint in a form that sings to us a cosmic melody and rhythm. Once we have drawn everything into the picture, we have spatially perceptible cosmic music; it is cosmic music that has become audible to spiritual hearing when the planetary movements have disappeared into a mist.

What we have drawn into our image is the bloodstream. Then we come to an organ such as the heart or lungs or those that absorb substances from the outside world or from the body itself, and at these points we must paint forms attached in a certain way to the blood vessels. Thus the heart, lungs, liver, kidneys, and stomach emerge. From cosmic music we insert the organs of secretion related to the blood stream, drawing them into our blood system in our drawing; the secretion can be added as well.

Let us take another step, from *inspiration* to *intuition*. Something very special arises from the cosmic music. Something develops that forms the tones together; one tone affects another, and we begin to hear *meaning* in this cosmic music. The cosmic music transforms into the speech of the whole cosmos; all that can be summed up in the term *cosmic speech* becomes audible. In earlier times this was referred to as the *cosmic word*. And because it becomes audible, we must now draw something else into our picture of the human being. This becomes obvious to us. We must proceed just as we do in ordinary writing, in which we express something through words formed by letters. In this way, we must express the meaning of individual cosmic words. We find that when we express these singular cosmic words and express them in our drawing, the muscular and skeletal structures of the human being arise in this picture. It is as though someone had told us something, and now we write it down; cosmic speech tells us something, and we draw it into our picture. We have found the whole human being through what the world beyond the Earth tells us.

But there is another, essentially different experience that comes to us though our observation. Let us return to the beginning of this whole process—the formation inscribed in the ether. While we practice this knowledge, the earthly element vanishes and remains only as a memory. If it did not remain as memory, we would be without any hold or support, which is essential when we want to know spirit. If spiritual knowledge excludes physical knowledge, it is no good. In physical life we must be able to remember, because if we could not recall our actions and experiences we would not be healthy. Likewise, within the realm of spiritual scientific knowledge we must always be able to recall what is present in the physical world. Thus, as we enter the formative activities of the planetary system, for the moment we forget entirely the other knowledge we had on Earth—all that we received from the wonderful achievements of physical science. No matter how thoroughly we studied natural science within the earthly sphere, in every instance of spirit knowledge we must each time reflect on and recall what we learned in the physical realm. We must continually remind ourselves that this is the solid ground we must stand upon. Nevertheless, it withdraws and becomes like a memory.

On the other hand, we now have another perception as something appears as the formative force in the planetary system. Compared to physical knowledge it is alive and vivid, just as immediate experience compares to a memory. A wholly different environment confronts us at this moment. The beings of the *third hierarchy* are present now—the hierarchy of the *archai, archangels,* and *angels.*[2] We see that the third hierarchy lives within this form. A new world arises now before us. We no longer have to say only that the cosmic archetype of the human form arose from the planetary system. Now we can say that the beings of the third hierarchy—the archai, archangels, and angels—are working and weaving this cosmic archetype of the human being.

In our earthly existence, it is possible to attain perception of the hierarchical world through suprasensory cognition. After death, every human being necessarily experiences such knowledge. And the better we prepare ourselves (as we can) during earthly existence, the easier this will be for us. But we must all go through it. On Earth, when we want to know our form, we can view ourselves or take a picture. After death, we do not have such means available to know our own or another's form. After death we must look out to the planets' formative activity and weaving; the planets reveal our form. There we recognize what I have described here as the human form. Woven into it, however, we see the angels, archangels, and archai of the third hierarchy working and weaving.

Let us progress upward. We have seen how the weaving life of angels, archangels, and archai is related to the forms of the human skin and the sensory organs placed within it; now we can learn more about our human relationship to the realm beyond Earth. First, however, we must be very clear about the fact that we talk

---

2. These hierarchies are described in greater detail in Rudolf Steiner's *Outline of Esoteric Science* and *The Spiritual Hierarchies: Reality and Illusion.*

differently here on Earth about a person's form having a certain shape. We speak of someone's forehead being formed in a particular way, of another having this or that shaped nose, while others have sad eyes or smiling eyes, and so on. And this is the end of it. But cosmic knowledge leads us to see the active weaving of the third hierarchy in all that contributes to the human form. In fact, the human form is not an earthly creation; the Earth merely provides the substance for the embryo, whereas the archai, archangels, and angels work in from the cosmos to build the human form.

We now advance further and perceive the confluence of planetary movements (reproduced as our nervous system and the secreting glands) and how they interweave with the beings of the *second hierarchy*—the *exusiai, kyriotetes,* and *dynamis.* And because the beings of the second hierarchy are connected with and work on the cosmic archetype of the human nervous and glandular systems, it later becomes our task after death—that is, some time after we have come to understand the human form in terms of its cosmic archetype—to ascend to the world of the second hierarchy. There we must come to understand how the physical human being (now recalled as a memory) was fashioned and created in the nervous and glandular systems by the exusiai, kyriotetes, and dynamis. Here we no longer regard the human being as a product of electrical forces, magnetism, and so on; rather we know how, as physical human beings, we were formed by beings of the second hierarchy.

Now we can go even farther, and by ascending to the sphere of cosmic music (cosmic melody and rhythm) we find yet another cosmic archetype of the human being. I have shown you how we draw this into our outline of the human being. But now we do not go any further in observing the hierarchies. It is again the second hierarchy—the exusiai, kyriotetes and dynamis—who are active here as well. But their activity here is different. It is difficult to express how their way of working on the nervous system differs from their work on the rhythmic blood system of the human being. To express this, we must describe it as follows. As they work on the nervous system, the beings of the second hierarchy gaze down to Earth; but when they work on the blood system, they look up. Both the nervous system and the blood system (as well as the organs connected with them) are created by the same hierarchy; but their gaze is turned toward the Earth in one instance and, in the other, upward to the spirit world and the heavens.

Finally, at the stage of *intuition* we see how the human muscular and skeletal systems are woven into being by the world of the cosmic word, or cosmic speech. Here we encounter the *first hierarchy*—the *seraphim, cherubim,* and *thrones.* We have thus reached the moment that corresponds approximately to the midpoint of life between death and a new birth. In my mystery plays, this is referred to as the "midnight hour of existence." We must then see that the beings of the first hierarchy weave and create all the elements of the human organism that enable us to move around in the world.

Consequently, as we view the human being with suprasensory cognition, we see a world of spiritual, cosmic beings behind everything. In our present age, in trying to understand the human being we usually begin by studying the skeletal system, although this makes little sense—even in a superficial sense—since the skeleton was formed and built up by the fluids of the human organism. The skeleton was not the first thing, but a residue of fluids, and it can be understood only in that sense. Nevertheless, what is the usual procedure? We must begin by learning the various parts of the skeleton—the bones of the upper arm, lower arm, the hands, the fingers, and so on. Most of us simply learn it all by rote. You know that most people learned it only by rote. It is the same with the muscles, though it is decidedly more difficult. When we come to the various organs, we learn about them in the same way, but there the concepts are largely thrown together pell-mell.

In all healthy minds, however, there is a longing to know more about what lies behind it all and to know something of the mystery of the world. If we made observations based on the actual facts about the human being, this would be the result: We would begin by studying the skin and the senses embedded in it, which leads to perception of the hierarchy of angels, archangels, and archai. Then, as we go further into the human being to the nervous and glandular systems, this leads us to the second hierarchy, the exusiai, kyriotetes, and dynamis. We stay with these same beings when we get to the blood system and the organs. And when it comes to what this system has built up, to what gives us the capacity for movement—the muscular and skeletal systems—we ascend to the first hierarchy and an understanding of these systems as the creation of the seraphim, cherubim, and thrones.

It is possible in this way to describe the ascending ranks of hierarchical beings, from the third to the second to the first. When we describe the influences pouring down upon Earth from beyond it, and in them we see the activities of the hierarchies, a marvelous picture arises before us. Gazing at the ranks of hierarchies, first we see the activity of the third hierarchical beings (angels, archangels, and archai); then we see the work of the second hierarchical beings (exusiai, kyriotetes, and dynamis) and how this all works and weaves together in the cosmos; and finally we see the beings of the first hierarchy (seraphim, cherubim, and thrones). Only now do we have a clear image of the human body before us; we have traced the order of the hierarchies to their activities, and, as we allow those activities to pass before the eye of the spirit, the human being stands before us.

As you can see, a mode of observation opens up at the very point where the other stops. Yet only this kind observation leads us beyond the gates of birth and death; there is no other that tells us about what stretches before birth or beyond death. All that can be described there becomes a matter of actual *experience*. In the coming lectures I will show how this becomes real experience. On Earth we are surrounded by the mineral, plant, and animal kingdoms and by what physical humankind accomplishes in the earthly sense. We direct our gaze toward all that arises from the mineral, plant, animal, and physical human being; likewise, once we have passed through the gate of death and live between death and a new birth, we gaze at activities of the spiritual world directed toward the human being, and we see the human being truly as a product of the activity and accomplishments of the higher spiritual hierarchies. We will also come to realize that, unless seen in this light, we cannot understand the forms and structures of the other beings of Earth.

Let me add something else in preparation for our coming lectures. Consider the animal; there is something about an animal that reminds us of the human form only in a limited sense. Why is this? An animal cannot duplicate the planetary form inscribed in the ether. Only human beings can become a replication of that form, because we strive toward the line that, as I mentioned, focuses the planetary image for us. If it were the destiny of human beings to remain children and never learn to walk but only crawl—which of course it is not—we would never be able to model our forms as human beings from the planetary forms. However, we must duplicate them, according to our human organization; we must grow into the planetary forms. But animals cannot do this; they must unfold their lives according to the *movements* of the planets; they replicate only planetary movements. You see this in every aspect of an animal's body.

Consider the skeleton of a mammal. The bones of the spine have a vortex shape, which faithfully replicates planetary movements. Regardless of the number of vertebrae in a snake, for example, each one physically copies planetary movements. The Moon, our nearest "planet," especially influences one part of the animal. This influence is particularly strong. The skeleton develops and forms the limbs; it then all works together in vortex formations. The other planets—Venus and Mercury—move in spiral formations. The Sun's influence, in a sense, finishes the skeletal structure.

We can even speak of a specific point in the spine where the Sun is especially active—the point where the spine tends to transform into the head structure, which displays a transformed spinal vertebra. Saturn and Jupiter work at the point where the bones of the spine rise and "puff out" (the description used by Goethe and Gegenbaur) to become skull bones. And, to understand the animal's skeletal structure we follow the direction of the skeleton from the back to front, going from Moon to Saturn. To understand the animal form, we cannot relate it to the form of the planets but to planetary *movements*. What we work into the glandular system as human beings, the animal works into its whole form and structure. Thus, we may say that the animal cannot arrange and order its being according to the form radiated by the planets, but begins directly with planetary movements.

The people of ancient times visualized these planetary movements as the paths of planets through the constellations of the zodiac. The ancients could describe the courses of Saturn and other planets as each traveled through the zodiac. Because of their knowledge of animals, they understood the relationship between animal forms and the zodiac (a word that means "animal circle"). The zodiac is correctly named as an animal circle, but for us the essential point is that the animal does not partake of the forms inscribed by the planets in the ether; only the human being does this. Human beings can do this because the human organism has assumed an upright posture. Consequently, the planetary form becomes an archetype in us, whereas we find only the planetary movements replicated in the animal.

Here we are presented with a spiritual, suprasensory image of the human being. Everything I have described—the skin, nervous system, cardiovascular system, musculature, and skeleton—initially contains only the image of *forces*. At conception, it is joined to the physical embryo and takes in the earthly forces and substances. This picture (purely spiritual but at the same time definite) fills itself with earthly substances and forces. As human beings, we come down to Earth formed and fashioned by the heavens. Initially, we are wholly suprasensory, right to our very bones. Then we unite with the embryo, the physical human seed; we fill it. At death, we let it fall away again and retain our spirit form as we pass through the gate of death.

In conclusion, let us observe the human being while passing through the gate of death. The physical form, which we can see by looking into a mirror or at a photograph, is no longer there. Nor are we interested in it at this point. We look toward the cosmic, archetypal image inscribed in the ether. During earthly life, this archetypal picture was anchored in our own ether body, but we did not perceive it. It is present within our physical being on Earth, but we do not notice it. Now, however, we see the reality of our own form. This image we see also shines out and radiates forces that have a very different effect. The forces flowing from this archetypal image have the same effect as a radiant body, except that it should be understood as *etheric*. The Sun shines physically; the cosmic image of the human being shines spiritually. And because this image is spiritual, it also has the power to illuminate other things. Here, in earthly life, those who have committed good or evil actions can be exposed to the Sun for as long as they like; the Sun's rays will light up their hair and other physical characteristics, but it will not illuminate their good or evil actions as qualities. The luminous image of our own form, which we experience after death, radiates a spiritual light that illuminates the morality of our actions. After death, we are confronted by this cosmic image, which illuminates our moral acts. During earthly life, this cosmic picture existed *within* us, where it could be heard faintly as our conscience. After death, we view it objectively; we know that we are seeing ourselves and that it *must* be there for us. We are unrelenting with ourselves after death, because this luminous image does not conform to any of the excuses we might make here to pardon our sins and emphasize our good actions. Rather, an inexorable judge radiates from us after death by directing a brilliant light upon the value of our acts. Our conscience becomes a cosmic impulse that works outside of us after death.

These are the matters that lead us from the earthly to the suprasensory human being. The earthly human being, who comes into existence at birth and passes away at death, can be understood through anthropology. The suprasensory human being, who is merely permeated by earthly substances so that the outer world can manifest, can be understood only through anthroposophy. This is the goal of this lecture course.

2. Interweaving Our Destinies

NOVEMBER, 14, 1923

MY DEAR FRIENDS, yesterday we tried to find the relationship between the human being and the cosmos. Through such studies we want to establish a basis for a deep, complete understanding of our suprasensory being. Today, I would take what we said yesterday a little further in a more "outer," suprasensory way. We will consider suprasensory human nature after a person has dispensed with the physical and etheric bodies—that is, while traveling the path between death and a new birth, after having passed through the gate of death. Today I will be more descriptive of what an externally imaginative approach perceives of this journey between dying and entering a new birth. This will provide a basis for understanding the human soul and spirit.

Nevertheless, we must be clear right from the beginning that it is really nonsense to speak of the physical human being apart from the human soul and spirit, because our physical aspect (the physical body as perceived in the world of the senses) is, in fact, thoroughly permeated and suffused by soul and spirit. Spiritual forces form our brow, our features and countenance, and all that is the human form. We should not be surprised, therefore, that those who possess a faculty for spiritual sight continue to speak of the form of the human being even after death. The truth is that *imaginative* cognition indeed sees that a person who has passed through death reveals a form. Compared to something physical, of course, it appears as no more than a kind of shadowy image; nevertheless, it is clear and very impressive. Initially, this form gives the impression of something external, because we have to imagine the human soul and spirit as moral and spiritual. But we find that we cannot develop a lasting and valid spiritual view of the suprasensory human being unless we first speak of these imaginations (or image forms) that we continue to wear, even after we have passed through the gate of death.

At death, we lay the physical body aside. We need not linger on what happens to it, since the particular way dissolution takes place is far less important than people believe. The dissolution of the physical body, whether it is cremated or simply decomposes, concerns only our fellow human beings and is not really important for our own life after death. So we must speak of the physical body, as it presents itself to sensory perception, as something that dissolves into outer nature and its forces.

Next, the etheric body also dissolves fairly soon after death (you know this from my presentation in *An Outline of Esoteric Science*). Once these two outer manifestations of the human being have been laid aside, something frees itself of them, which have acted as enveloping sheaths (though the word *sheath* is not quite accurate). Those endowed with the appropriate *imaginative* cognition perceive the nature of what is released after death from these two sheaths; it is a form that, initially, resembles the human physical form, in a certain sense. But this *spirit form*, as I will call it, is constantly changing. I have described the life between death and a new birth often and from widely varied perspectives, because this is the only way to develop an adequate concept of it. Today I plan to speak of it from yet another specific perspective. We must add this to what has been presented at various other times to get a complete picture.

This human spirit form changes constantly. Indeed, it will always continue to transform, so that we can really characterize it appropriately only when we say that it completely becomes a "physiognomy," or countenance. To the *imaginative* vision of an initiate or one who has passed through the gate of death, a physiognomy, as it were, appears. This countenance is the whole human being, not merely a part. The whole human being appears, according to the physiognomy in spirit form, so that this physiognomy expresses the inner moral and spiritual nature of the human being. After death a bad person will look different from a good person. One who has made strenuous efforts during earthly life will not appear the same as one whose life was thoughtless or superficial.

But all this expresses itself in a way that is more than countenance. Indeed, one's countenance loses much of the characteristic impressed upon it during physical life. What it retains tends to become less and less defined, and other aspects of the body, by contrast, become very expressive, especially inside where the lungs are. The physiognomic form of the location of the lungs during physical life reveals the permanent qualities of one's character. The entire chest region assumes a definite physiognomic appearance within the spirit form after death, and it reveals whether a person was courageous or timid, whether one approached life with boldness and bravery or invariably shrank from the blows of life, and so on.

The arms and hands have a special capacity for expression after death; the biography of a person can be read from them between birth and death. This may be seen most clearly by a thoughtful observer in the hands, which even in physical life are full of meaning and very revealing in their countenance. In physical life, we are very expressive in the way we move our fingers, the way we hold out our hands to others when we meet them, whether we shake hands with the finger tips or press warmly with the whole hand. We can also learn a great deal from how people move and shape their hands in everyday life and work. Such things usually go unnoticed, but people become much more interesting when we observe how they hold and move their hands and fingers, because they reveal themselves this way. After death this is even more so; an individual's life history can be read in the arms and hands. This is also true of other organs. Everything expresses itself physiognomically. After death human beings wear their moral and spiritual physiognomy.

Yesterday we talked of how people are shaped by the cosmos and appear before us formed, and about how this form embedded in the skin and the sensory organs expresses what the cosmos has inscribed into the cosmic ether. But this form—bound by the skin and familiar to us in earthly life as a person's form—becomes the physical expression of our moral and spiritual physiognomy; and it continues this way for quite some time.

As human beings enter this way into the new life, they meet the others with whom they had, in earthly life, a community of spirit, mind, and heart. At this point, pretence is no longer an option for them. The true nature of each person and their feeling toward others is faithfully represented in the physiognomy just described. During this period of life after death we live with those we were connected with through destiny in the previous earthly life or in some other earthly life. (This follows the "period of trial," which I do not intend to consider today.[1]) They come to know one another thoroughly. At this initial stage, however, we come to know one another completely by witnessing the physiognomic forms I have described. And what we experience during this period is precisely this intimacy with those to whom we are related by destiny. You must try to imagine how close and intimate this mutual scrutiny really is. Perhaps the words sound somewhat ordinary, but they *express* the reality. Each human

---

1. See the afterword, pp. 116ff and Rudolf Steiner, *Theosophy*, Anthroposophic Press, Hudson, NY, 1994, "The Three Worlds," especially pp. 118ff.

being stands fully revealed to the other, along with the whole meaning of their common destiny. This is how we encounter one another and live together.

Also during this period of existence, those who have become a physiognomy come to know the beings of the third hierarchy—angels, archangels, and archai. These beings are *always* physiognomy; it is their permanent nature. They issued from the cosmic beings of the higher hierarchies, manifesting their whole soul and spiritual nature as spirit forms, thus making it perceptible to imagination. So, in addition to keeping company with those who are connected with us by destiny, we experience the beings of the third hierarchy during this time.

Of course, the display of all those with whom we are connected by destiny is full of variety. Among them, for example, are some who would have preferred that we were on the opposite sides of the world; nevertheless, they are connected to us by destiny. We know exactly what they thought of and what they actually did to us. There is great variety in these encounters. And, like radiant sun figures, beings of the third hierarchy are present as we move among these wandering forms. Of course, the words I use only suggest the reality of this, but there is no alternative to earthly language. But when we say that, during this period after death, we meet those with whom we are bound by destiny, this is the *reality*.

Strangely enough, we are able to understand only those with whom we are connected by destiny. To a certain extent, those with whom we are not connected by destiny are invisible to us. We have no way of reading their moral and spiritual physiognomy; we do not notice them, nor are we able to, because only connections of destiny give us the power to see. We would see very little here on Earth if it were our fate to see with physical eyes as we do after death, because here people love to observe in a passive way, merely allowing objects to shine into their eyes. In our current era of civilization, people are not very inclined to arouse themselves to wakefulness in regard to their surroundings. Many of those who are especially fond of movies and look only for impressions to which they can passively surrender would, if they had the kind of vision we have after death, not be able to see other human beings at all on Earth. This is because after death our ability to see other human souls depends entirely on *attentiveness,* which is implanted in us at that point by our connection with others through destiny.

During the first period of life after death we learn about one another and about how human souls are received into the spiritual world by beings of the third hierarchy. We witness the joy of the angels, archangels, and archai for human beings who come into the spiritual world in the form I have described. Or we perceive how little joy they experience in relation to them. We observe the effects human souls have on the beings of the hierarchies that are closest to them in the invisible world.

Then another period begins. Human beings who have been coming to know one another and have been continually gazing at one another now begin to understand one another in a way that is a part of our life after death. They begin to understand in a spiritual way the moral, spiritual physiognomies.

In the first period after death we really live in nothing but memories. We live with those to whom we are connected, though we live very much in the present. We live, move, and act amid all that takes place among human beings and the beings of the third hierarchy, but in a kind of remembrance of earthly life.

Then a period starts when we begin to gain spiritual understanding and comprehend (as comprehension must occur in the spiritual world) the meaning that human moral and spiritual physiognomies have for one another. We come to understand our fellow human beings, and thus we can say that a certain physiognomy indicates events of destiny that one has shared with a certain individual, and so on. We experience this during the first period right after death by viewing our associations according to destiny. Now, however, in the second period, our experience tells us that, having lived our life together as revealed by the mutual understanding of our physiognomies, our future together must now follow a particular course. We begin to comprehend a possible future course of progress for our common destiny, and we begin to get a sense of how our relationships begun during earthly life can be developed. We see in perspective how the "threads of destiny" form in the future, threads of common destiny revealed in the moral and spiritual physiognomies. This experience becomes increasingly intimate—indeed, so intimate that the souls grow together.

As the soul proceeds during this phase of existence, the most expressive part of our being on Earth—the head—gradually disappears. It dissolves into a kind of spiritual mist. To the same extent that the head disappears, the features of the moral, spiritual physiognomy also change. The features alter, and something appears that points from the past into the future. At this point, one is placed into the spirit of the planetary movements—that is, the spirit of the forces of the planetary system. As a result, those who belong together approach the spiritual Sun existence at a specific time after death. The planetary forces bring them into the spiritual Sun existence; all the experiences they have shared along with the seeds for future experience are carried with them into the spiritual Sun.

From the perspective of real knowledge, it is childish to conceive of the Sun as a ball of gas out there in the universe; this is only the view the Sun reveals to Earth. When we look at it with eyes of the spirit or soul (which we have after death), and view it from out in the great universe, the Sun is revealed as a spiritual being, or rather, as an assembly of spiritual beings. And mixed among those spiritual beings are human souls who bring to the Sun's spiritual existence not only their own individual spiritual essence but also their common destinies. This whole "system" of human souls shines out into the cosmos, along with judgments the beings of the second and third hierarchies have passed on them.

The only way we can correctly conceive of the Sun from any earthly viewpoint is this: As we observe the Sun from the Earth's surface, it does indeed appear like a shining, radiant ball. We could make a drawing of it. We usually think that, if we could ascend in a balloon and inspect the Sun from high above the Earth, it would appear exactly the same as it does when seen from Earth. But this is not the case. If we wanted to make a picture—a sensorially perceptible image of how the Sun looks to spiritual vision—we would have to show spirit radiating from the Sun into the vast expanses of the cosmos. From Earth we see only the aspect of the Sun that shines toward Earth. Now, however, something appears to spiritual vision that gradually becomes a spiritually audible perception; it becomes an element in the music of the cosmos, and it is something quite magnificent. But this element has been experienced by humankind in the past, and it is experienced also after death. This is all carried into the Sun existence, and it then radiates into the cosmos. When this happens, the human beings there have already assumed the form of the Sun to a certain extent in their spirit form.

These words sound contradictory, but we must describe the facts as they correspond to reality. After passing through the gate of death, all that was human physiognomy, or spirit form, becomes round, and when human beings arrive in the Sun (in the spiritual sense) they have in fact become a sphere of spirit. Each human being has become a spiritual sphere. And the cosmos is reflected in this spirit sphere. To the degree that our whole being has become a sensory organ of spirit, the impressions we receive are no longer earthly. One completely becomes a "spiritual eye," and this spiritual eye receives an impression of the entire cosmos;

we feel united with the whole wide universe. Our earthly being is now experienced as external to us. But as we reflect the whole universe in ourselves, as in a spiritual eye, we feel united with the destinies we have experienced both individually and with others.

After living for a while in this period of existence, we move gradually into the sphere of the first hierarchy, that of the seraphim, cherubim, and thrones. We unite with the first hierarchy. First we united with the third hierarchy where we moved among human beings bound to us by destiny, moving in our moral and spiritual physiognomy. Then we were carried by the planetary forces into the spiritual Sun existence, where we united with the second hierarchy. But then we were still outside the first. Now, once our own Sun existence has made us feel at one with the whole cosmos, we unite with the first hierarchy of seraphim, cherubim, and thrones. And at this point we begin to be able to become interested in more than only those with whom we are connected by past destiny. Other souls appear now for the first time in our life between death and rebirth, and they enter our sphere of destiny. We now begin to see human beings other than those previously tied to us by destiny, souls with whom we will be connected by destiny in future incarnations. Under the influence of the seraphim, cherubim, and thrones, however, we begin to notice that the forms of those with whom we were already connected by destiny are changing in powerful ways that correspond to the extent of our connections.

First, I will describe this more externally. When we physically observe someone walking, we see first one foot move to the front, then the other, and thus that person moves forward. As we watch, we see what we might call a series of momentary "snapshots." But to those who use imagination to observe a person in the existence after death, the legs appear to assume a form with every step that contains that individual's destiny, the destiny that is currently being experienced and was molded during earthly life.

And destiny is carried not only in the legs, but the arms also bear the significance of our destiny—the effects, both good and bad, of what we did with our hands to others. The way we move displays an impulse toward justice, how it is brought into the world and included as a part of our destiny. Similarly, in the blood stream we can see the inner destiny we create through our moods and inner responses to life. These revelations of destiny can be seen for quite some time after one has entered this realm of existence; one can still observe them in the form of the limbs and, except for the head and chest, in other human forms.

On Earth, the sight of someone walking by with no head or chest would be very unpleasant, but in the sphere between death and a new birth it is very different. There everything is changed into morality and spirit. What we see there is much more powerful than seeing any human head on Earth. Those who are connected by destiny have such experiences during their spiritual Sun existence, which in my mystery plays I call "cosmic midnight." Depending on how much they are really connected, human beings work together to transform the nature of what they were in the previous earthly life. With spiritual sight we can witness what happens here in detail. We see, for example, how the leg is changed into the form of the lower jaw in the next earthly life, and how the arms and hands are transformed into the upper jaw and the nerves in that area. You must understand, of course, that this is all seen through spiritual perception, which can watch the whole lower human being change into the upper part.

A human being does not effect this change alone but through all who belong together, to the degree that they are connected by destiny. They work on one another. This mutual work leads to spiritual relationships that cause human beings to find one another and come together in earthly life. Such spiritual relationships, brought about in the life between death and rebirth, unite us with some degree of intimacy. It is indeed true that the spiritual form of the head as it will appear in the next incarnation is built by the mutual activities of those who are united by destiny. This work is done in the spirit land, and its meaning and significance are certainly not less than our work on Earth; on the contrary, they are more so.[2]

So you see, just as we can use images taken from earthly life to picture what happens to us between birth and death, similarly we can describe in concrete detail all that happens to us between death and a new birth; we can picture it all very concretely. The transformation in the limbs and metabolic and blood system is marvelous and awe-inspiring. Midway between death and a new birth, however, it is our human moral and spiritual qualities that are transformed. And what emerges from those transformations is the sound of cosmic music. This human form is fashioned after the Sun and reflects the whole universe; it reveals the outer form of the human being as cosmic tone. One does not (comparatively speaking) see a visual representation of the human being. Instead, one is presented with a representation of the transformed lower human being as cosmic sound.

And as this continues to progress ever further, one becomes a part of the cosmic word itself. The initial blend of melodies and harmonies now becomes articulated aspects of the cosmic word. Our nature becomes such that we "speak" our own being as if from the cosmos. Consequently, there is a period between death and a new birth when our being becomes, in fact, "spirit word." This is not merely a word of a few syllables but one of infinite expression; it speaks not only the whole of humankind in general, but also the whole of that particular individuality. During this period between death and a new birth, one mysteriously knows and sends a revelation into the cosmos revealing the nature of the human being that is perceptible to divine, spiritual beings.

---

2. See afterword, p. 130.

When the human individuals work on one another to transform the lower parts of their form into the upper (the upper most parts have gradually dissolved), and when the foundation for their future association has been established according to their past relationships, it is as though a spiritually sculpted element of feeling were being shaped. One takes up this spiritually sculpted element and works it, transforming it into a musical sound and, finally, into speech.

During the first stage after death, we move among the spiritual physiognomies of those we are connected with by destiny; we witness those physiognomies. We become aware of one another and come to know one another in a spiritual form according to moral and spiritual qualities. During this first stage, however, it is only a kind of seeing—it is no more than seeing, though the human souls bring it together in an intimate way. Then a period begins that I described as a mutual understanding, in which we gaze with understanding deeply into the inner nature of one another, recognizing how the future will connect with the past as destiny develops. Next, a process of transformation unfolds from this, in which one works on another through deep knowledge, and where the spiritual sculpting is transformed into musical sound followed by speech.

Now we go to something more than understanding; we speak our own warm, "creation word" to one another. On Earth we utilize a speech organ to talk to one another about what we know. The physical body provides the basis for what we say, and living within it—as a fleeting element to which a higher element has been added—are the ordinary words we use. We use our vocal organs to express ourselves to one another, and this shuts off and eliminates what lives behind our merely physical aspect. Imagine how it would be if what we say—what flows into fleeting words— were not only the expression of our very being but were at the same time our being. This gives you a picture of how human beings distinguish between and reveal themselves to one another midway between death and a new birth. Word encounters word; articulated word meets articulated word; inwardly enlivened word meets inwardly enlivened word. But the human beings themselves *are the words*, and chiming together they harmoniously sound the spoken word being. Impermeability does not exist there; they indeed live together, and the word that each one really is comes to life in the word that is the being of the other. And links of destiny are formed there that continue to work into the next incarnation, and these express themselves as sympathy or antipathy when these human beings meet again. These feelings of sympathy or antipathy reflect what we said to one another in the spirit land midway between death and a new birth. There we talked with one another, and we ourselves were being spoken. On Earth we feel a vague reflection of this when we meet one another again.

This is approximately the way we would have to describe the sense of our experience on Earth with others: as reverberations of what we each were in the creative word, speaking our being in the life between death and a new birth. That is when we exist for one another in the truest sense. When we live for one another on Earth, it is a projection of spirit onto Earth of that true togetherness.

After we have lived through that period of time, we enter another. We begin to separate gradually from the beings of the first hierarchy (the seraphim, cherubim, and thrones), and we return again to the realm of the second hierarchy and the forces that planets exert on one another. This is where perceptions of the universe arise, perceptions that had been less direct before, because we were able to follow them only in other beings. The cosmos now begins to arise before us as an *outer* universe. We learn also of our mutual relationships with beings whose destinies are not connected to us. We learn of our connections with those human beings who first appeared during the middle period between death and rebirth.

This occurs when we reenter the planetary spheres and connect with the beings of the second hierarchy. We have been with them before, but now the connection is different, because the first hierarchy have gradually faded from sight and are eventually no longer present. Spirit seeds are found there for the pliable form of the human being, for the new human chest and limbs. The human being gradually forms and rebuilds a preparatory human form.

What we spoke as our own being in cosmic word becomes cosmic again, and the pictorial sculpture of our being grows from the music of the spheres. Now we approach the moment when we are ready to connect with the embryonic seed provided by a mother and father; we simply join with it. There is a spiritual form that descends from the spiritual world into physical existence, and this is the actual human being, whereas the embryo offered to us exists only so that we can connect and permeate ourselves with earthly matter.

Our life between death and a new birth is rich in meaning. The work we do there is the interaction between ourselves and beings of the higher realms. The whole outer nature of our life between death and a new birth is completely different from the nature and essence of life here on Earth.

Let us take our study further and increase our understanding of our suprasensory human nature. To do this, we must become clear about a few things. First, we live in the physical world of Earth; here we perceive the outer world through our senses. We must say that we perceive things that are sensorially perceptible and physical. In earthly life we perceive only what is physically perceptible.

Beyond this world there is a second to which our ether body belongs. It imbues and permeates the physical body. This world is initially imperceptible to our physical faculties of perception; it is not physical but *supraphysical.* Bordering our perceptible, physical world, therefore, is one that is imperceptible and supraphysical. This is the next world beyond our own, and within it live the third hierarchy beings (angels, archangels, and archai). This other world is imperceptible to those who live in a physical, earthly incarnation and have not developed spiritual sight. It is not physical, but its activity does manifest in the physical world.

There is also a third adjoining world. This world is also not physical, and in this respect it is similar to the etheric world. It is also supraphysical. But, oddly enough, it *is perceptible*—it can be perceived from our world. Now we have come to the characteristic of a world that reaches into our world and is perceptible; but it is also supraphysical. Consequently, we cannot explain its true nature. What we receive in sunlight, for example, belongs to this world that is supraphysical but perceptible. All the spirit beings who populate the Sun are supraphysical, yet they are perceptible to us on Earth. It is nonsense to think that sunlight is only what physicists imagine. The light of the Sun is a manifestation of the Sun beings. Sun beings are perceptible but appear to us in a form we cannot interpret. The light of the stars, the moon, the Sun, and other forms of light are also perceptible, but people do not have the right understanding of the beings behind it. Here we have a world that is perceptible but supraphysical and borders the world that is physically perceptible. It is very important to understand the characteristics of these different worlds:

1. Our earthly world—perceptible and physical.

2. The second world, bordering the first. Angels, archangels, and archai live in this realm. It is imperceptible and supraphysical; it is the dwelling of the third hierarchy but also that of human beings between death and a new birth while associated with the third hierarchy.

3. The third world is perceptible and supraphysical. It is the dwelling of the second hierarchy.

And finally:

4. An imperceptible physical world.

With the fourth, we have a complete list of all possible worlds: 1) perceptible and physical; 2) imperceptible and supraphysical; 3) perceptible and supraphysical; 4) imperceptible and physical. This fourth world is imperceptible and yet physical. How can we visualize it? It is in our midst and present physically, and yet it is imperceptible.

Consider, for example, the fact that your leg is heavy when you lift it off the ground; the force of gravity affects it. The force of gravity acts physically, but it is imperceptible to ordinary sensory perception. You experience this force of gravity inwardly but, in itself, it is imperceptible to our physical senses. The same is true of certain other phenomena. You experience them within, but with feelings you cannot explain. An earlier, more instinctive spiritual science knew this as the "mercurial" tendency, which strives toward the form of a drop. You always contain it within as the protein your bodies use. Again, this is something physical, but in its own configuration. You see, there is a living process of combustion within you. It acts physically and lives in your will, though you are unaware of it. It is imperceptible and physical. The first hierarchy beings (seraphim, cherubim, and thrones) are within this world, the realm of the *imperceptible and physical*.

And now we come to something strange. When we pass through the gate of death, first we enter the imperceptible and supraphysical. We disappear from this world. At the second stage we enter the sphere of the second hierarchy, the perceptible and supraphysical. During this phase of existence we comprehend our destinies in the flowing, flooding light element of the Sun and stars. One who has learned to gaze into the essence of this light does not merely look thoughtlessly into the expanses of the universe—the spheres of the Sun and stars; one knows that, within this flooding, flowing light, threads of human destiny are woven. This is the realm of the perceptible and supraphysical, in which those who have died—the so-called dead—live.

Human beings again achieve the metamorphosis that prepares them to return to the Earth, where they appear. But the world they wander between death and a new birth, the realm of the imperceptible and physical, is involved in the gravitational process, the phosphoric and mercurial processes of formation (and we will gradually come to understand how these develop). First we are withdrawn from life into the invisible, then we return imperceptibly to be withdrawn again so we may prepare for a future perceptible and physical life on Earth. The path between death and new birth leads from the perceptible and physical life on Earth through the other conditions to the *imperceptible physical* Earth life during the "midnight hour" of our existence. After that, we make our way back and reenter physical existence on Earth.

This has been merely a preliminary outline, which we intend to elaborate in detail in the lectures to come. As you see, we cannot be content with generalities and abstractions about life between death and a new birth. We can point out, for example, how we come invisibly to Earth between death and a new birth to prepare for our future life in the visible world. Just think how our understanding of life on Earth is deepened when we know how spirit lives and is present within physical, earthly existence at the cosmic midnight. Besides the physically embodied human beings among us here in earthly existence, there are spiritual essences continually wandering among us with vitality, who are at the midnight hour of their existence between death and rebirth. We are unaware of them, because their present earthly existence is at the midnight hour rather than at noon.

We will look into the meaning of all this in the next lecture.

3. Through the Spheres

afternoon, NOVEMBER, 17, 1923

IN OUR FIRST LECTURE we tried to form an idea of how earthly humankind is related to beings and forces in the realms beyond Earth. In the second lecture we considered, from a certain standpoint, the human passage through the spiritual world between death and a new birth. Now in this lecture I want to go a little farther, adding to what was said before. As our study proceeds, we will conclude our discussions with a harmonious, self-contained picture.

We have seen that human beings pass through the gate of death and enter the suprasensory realm. There they reveal themselves to imagination as in spiritual form. Please understand that perception of spirit is very different from perceiving an object in the world of senses. For example, those endowed with spiritual vision will tell you that when they perceived this or that, they could not tell you its size and so on. Phenomena of the spiritual realm are not spatial the way material objects are to the physical eye. Nevertheless, if we want to describe them, we can do so in such a way that they resemble an image seen physically, or some other earthly terminology might be used to describe it. So I ask you to consider this while I describe such things.

When a human being has passed through the gate of death, the spirit form of the head gradually fades. On the other hand, the rest of one's form becomes a kind of physiognomy. This countenance expresses, for example, how good or bad or how wise or foolish a person was in earthly life. Everything we can hide in the sensory world—where villains are able to maintain absolutely innocent faces—can no longer be hidden once we pass through the gate of death. Your face cannot hide it, because one's face fades immediately, and the rest of one's form becomes a physiognomy that allows nothing to be denied. The point here is that, after we have passed into the spiritual world, our whole relationship to the universe changes. We must realize that the faculty of thinking (especially the kind of abstract thinking we consider so important on Earth) has absolutely no value in the spiritual world. The faculty that uses the head as its apparatus is completely without value in the spiritual world; we cannot use it there. We must abandon the kind of thinking, of which we are so proud, through which we develop our concepts of material phenomena. Philosophers exist only on Earth because it is precisely philosophical, abstract thinking that is left behind.

The further we penetrate the spiritual world, the more completely our soul life becomes perception, the kind of sight whereby the thoughts underlying things are conveyed to us along with seeing. On Earth we develop thoughts; in the spirit world, the things themselves reveal thoughts, which come to us. Thought is accomplished there through perception. And this is true of not only thought—indeed, *all* of our experience in the spiritual world comes to us through perception.

In the sense-perceptible world, we have certain references to help us describe the spiritual in which we live between death and a new birth. In the realm of the senses we see stars and the planets of our system, and they reveal only their outer nature to our senses. Their inner reality is very different; they are the gathering of spiritual beings who have come together in diverse ways where stars appear in the heavens. When we observe a star with our physical eyes, there is, in fact, a community of spiritual beings at that place in the cosmos. The physical star we see shows us only the direction—a signpost, or chart. Conventional scientific descriptions of stars have very little meaning, because they deal only with those signposts, or charts to orient our vision. When we see a star somewhere in the sky, it indicates the location of a community of spiritual beings.

We go first to the Moon sphere after death—that is, to the region of spiritual beings who dwell within that sphere.[1] What sort of beings are they? If you have read my *Outline of Esoteric Science*, you know that the Moon has not always been out in the heavens where it is now.[2] The Moon sphere is characterized by strange facts. For example, it is very peculiar that conventional textbooks do not mention that the Moon comes closer to Earth each year. Because this fact is not in textbooks, most people are unaware of it. It is true nevertheless. The Moon was not always out in the cosmos; indeed, at one time the Moon and its substance existed *within* the Earth (you can read about this in *An Outline of Esoteric Science*). The Moon split off from Earth and went out into space. Consequently, the Moon as such became a dwelling for spiritual beings during earthly evolution.

And who are those spiritual beings? I have often described in books and lectures the great primordial teachers who lived among humankind during the very early times of Earth's evolution.[3] When we recall that ancient time with true understanding, it fills us with deep reverence for the marvelous wisdom that human beings on Earth were given long ago by those great, superior human teachers. Those first teachers of earthly humanity were not human themselves, but were higher than humanity in the evolutionary continuum. They did not appear physically in

1. See afterword, pp. 116-120.
2. See *An Outline of Esoteric Science*, pp. 165–197.
3. See especially chapter 6, "Cosmic and Human Evolution, Now and in the Future" in *An Outline of Esoteric Science*.

the Mysteries but in etheric bodies, which they have for the most part set aside since that time, dwelling today in astral bodies. These primordial teachers left Earth and went into the cosmos to the Moon. The celestial body we know as the Moon is thus a dwelling in the cosmos for the primordial teachers of humanity. To coarse perception, the Moon's outer aspect merely reflects sunlight. But to finer perception, the Moon mirrors a myriad of cosmic forces. But the cosmic forces reflected down to Earth are related to all that is subhuman in us as human beings—that is, what we share with animal nature. Strangely enough, as a result the Moon unites those higher spiritual beings who were once primordial teachers with the animal forces in human nature.

This is the first realm that human beings enter after passing through the gate of death; our first experiences occur there. Imagine as vividly as possible how, in our moral—or immoral—physiognomy, we enter that realm of physical and spiritual radiation from the Moon, and how we initially see ourselves and others in those physiognomies. We do not perceive the beings of that region with our physical eyes, but with a feeling, or touching, at a distance.

Let me try to describe this to you. Imagine that we come up to another being in this region. Our physiognomy is pliant and soft, so to speak. When we are near another being, we try to assume a physiognomy similar to the one revealed by the other. But if one who had been a scoundrel during earthly life were to arrive in the moon sphere and attempt to assume the physiognomy and experience of one who was truly virtuous in order to feel what it is like to be that person, such an attempt would fail. A scoundrel can produce only a scoundrel's physiognomy, nothing else.

Thus, you can see that, for a certain period of time after death, we perceive only those human beings who had a similar moral nature as our own during earthly life. This is the first impression of *judgment* that we experience. We actually experience these events as the administration of strict justice. This exerts a harsh justice; there is a constant impression that you are exactly like those you perceive. You move only among those like yourself and see no other kinds of beings; one simply does not perceive them at all.

The particular forces of this moon environment are such that the angeloi with their beautiful forms are not permitted to associate immediately with human beings. The Moon was cast off by the Earth; it is the cosmic body that Earth ejected into cosmic space, though it is also true that the great holy primordial teachers of the human race went with it. But ahrimanic forces are near its present isolated place in the cosmos; ahrimanic forms may be seen there. Consequently, when you see another human being with an immoral physiognomy, you have the impression that you are seeing yourself with those ahrimanic forms, and, in despair, you realize that you actually resemble those forms that appear there. We do not yet perceive the angeloi, because we are inwardly unlike their forms. Thus we perceive other human beings in certain evil shapes, and can see how similar they are to ahrimanic forms. That is our second impression in the moon sphere—our close resemblance to ahrimanic forms. This is another very effective form of judgment after death.

Our third experience is that we cannot avoid the distinct impression that the good primordial teachers of humanity are present in the first region through which we must roam. This impression is unavoidable, because there is a strange relationship between the ahrimanic beings we encounter (as described) and those earliest teachers of humanity. From the perspective of human beings, of course, it is understandable that, when it comes to judging the sort of things I am speaking of, they tend to have the same attitude as that famous king of Spain. When he was shown a map of the stars and their movements, as well as the whole solar system, he found it too difficult to understand. He said that the universe was far too complicated and that, if God had allowed him to create it, he would have made a much simpler universe. It's not surprising that many people think much like this and always want to correct the divine, universal cosmic plan. Human beings believe they are extremely capable when it comes to understanding. Indeed, there was once a philosopher who said, "Give me matter, and I will make a universe." This was Kant. It's a good thing he was not given any matter—he would have made something appalling with it.

Similarly, when people hear about ahrimanic beings, they fail to understand why such beings did not give up all hope long ago of conquering the Earth spirits. Human beings know very well that ahrimanic beings will not be victorious. Ahriman, however, is unaware of this and works unceasingly for victory. Through his efforts to win, a peculiar relationship arises between ahrimanic beings (who belong primarily to the Moon sphere) and the wise, primordial teachers of humanity; there is terrible flattery on the part of ahrimanic beings toward the teachers of humanity whom they would like to win over to their side. After all, what are those ahrimanic beings trying to do? Their goal is to arrest earthly development at a certain point and prevent it from further progress. It is always Ahriman who says, "Human beings have brought their evolution thus far; now they must stop and go no further. I want them to harden into their present condition and continue on their cosmic journey as ossified creatures, not as evolving human beings." Ahrimanic beings "whisper" these things into our ears every night. It is what they want to happen to the whole Earth; they wish to stop its evolution at a certain point.

Now consider the great primordial teachers of humanity in this sense. They left behind on Earth the ancient, primordial wisdom taught in the old mysteries, but it has dimmed through the ages and is no longer understood. The teaching of this ancient wisdom could not continue, because if we had continued to receive it we would not have progressed. Above all, we would not have gained the possibility of freedom; we would not have free will. Wisdom could speak only to human instinct, not to clear self-awareness. Consequently, for the benefit of humanity, these great teachers withdrew at a particular point in time.

If the primordial teachers had never lived on Earth, humanity would never have found the beginning of its evolution. But once they had provided the catalyst for independent, human evolution, they left Earth and went to the community of the Moon. The ahrimanic beings did all they could to hold the primordial teachers on Earth and to keep the instinctive nature of wisdom as it was, and even today they still believe that when human beings pass through the gate of death and arrive in the moon sphere, something may yet be achieved. So they continually try to flatter and entice those teachers to approach those who have just died. But they cannot attain this goal, especially in relation to those human beings who wear an evil physiognomy. Nevertheless, ahrimanic beings continuously work on human beings in the Moon sphere and taunt them by pointing to the primordial teachers and saying, "That was all once there; it was yours!" Human beings who wear evil features must now pass through a third experience. The ahrimanic beings describe the primordial teachers to them, but because of their nature, they cannot see those teachers and merely stare into a void.

Again, this is a very significant, judgmental impression for human beings. Then a feeling begins to weigh heavily on the soul, because one is unable to see those who gave humankind its starting point; one feels repudiated and rejected. This powerfully penetrating experience comes to those without a physiognomy that expresses good.

These are the three necessary impressions for those who have a physiognomy of evil when entering the world beyond the gate of death. Of course, one must bear in mind that no one is completely good; after all, there is much that is evil in the very best of us. Consequently, it is the fate of a great number of human beings to experience, to some degree, the impressions I have described. But the more we can assume the physiognomy of the good after death, the more we are able to see those whom we resemble through goodness, and the less we will be aware of ahrimanic beings.

Now what I have been saying about ahrimanic forms gradually disappears from the picture, and we develop a more penetrating awareness of the angelic forms that then enter our sphere. Through this, forces enter into us with which we permeate our being; these are primarily forces of will. After death, our main faculties are not thinking or reflection, but the will. Will becomes feeling, or sensing; it becomes the whole realm of life. You see, if we are to have any perception at all, we must exert our will to cause our forms to resemble what we want to see. Consequently, we must *will*. In other words, we must become similar to what we would like to perceive. Above all, it is the will that is developed after we pass through the gate of death. And the impressions of good and evil I described in relation to the Moon sphere also work on the will.

The next sphere that human beings enter is that of Mercury.[4] Thus far we have adapted our physiognomy (often at the cost of great suffering) to the powers and forces of the suprasensory world. We have laid aside the physiognomy of evil and gradually come to resemble the forms of angels, archangels, and archai. For many, this process is often slow. Nevertheless, we enter the sphere of Mercury, where the beings of the third hierarchy dwell. We must live there among them and experience what I described.

In this region we gradually understand what had previously been only perception—more or less blind perception; but it worked very powerfully on the human will. In the Mercury sphere, we gradually come to understand everything we have perceived.

---

4. See afterword, pp. 120ff.

In our time, those who investigate this through *imagination* perceive something tragic, because the way we find our way to the Mercury sphere after death depends somewhat on whether or not we were materialists here on Earth; it depends on whether we rejected, in thought and action, everything of a suprasensory nature or came to understand such matters here. One who rejected all that transcends the material realm during earthly life now confronts the beings in the Mercury sphere with relatively little understanding.

And this is also true for materialists in the next region. Beings there may also be classified as angeloi, archangeloi, and archai, but somewhat higher in their development. In the realm of Venus, materialists confront those beings without understanding, because the beings there radiate cosmic forces of love. This region will be the strangest and most foreign to those who failed to acquire a capacity for love on Earth. In the realm of Venus the loving forces, which would otherwise pour over those who had acquired a capacity to love here on Earth, now become *wrathful* forces in those who, on Earth, harbored hate, whether consciously or unconsciously. It is the mystery of our journey through the Venus sphere that those who bring forces of hatred with them from the Earth now experience Venus's forces of love arising from their will and changing into forces of fury and anger. They see themselves manifested there in a way that motivates them to admit that it must all be softened, mitigated, and made harmonious with the cosmos. Essentially, it is always the *will* that receives special care and nurturing in the Venus sphere. And the will is grounded in the limb and metabolic system in the lower part of earthly human beings. As we have seen, this is the aspect of the human being that becomes the entire appearance after death; it is therefore the will grounded there that is now expressed in this way.

Also during this time we continue to develop gradually so that we begin to resemble the beings of the spiritual cosmos, and we eventually enter the sphere of the Sun. Everything I have described is also involved in this (but this also gets into other viewpoints that are new, which we must take up later). The forces of the Sun sphere work primarily on all that which we have on Earth as a reflection of *feeling*. When we physically look up at the Sun, it reveals only its outer aspect. Inwardly, the Sun is the great cosmic gathering place for all of the spiritual beings who, from this center, guide and direct earthly destinies of human beings and all that is a part of Earth. Above all, the Sun is the community of beings of the second hierarchy (exusiai, kyriotetes, and dynamis). When we enter the Sun realm, we are met by everything I described in the previous lecture. Whereas before entering the Sun sphere we lived only among those human beings with whom we are linked by destiny, now others approach us as well. Our "circle of acquaintances" (if I may use such an expression) grows larger. All this takes place now in the Sun sphere.

It is also here in this Sun sphere that an especially strong inner experience arises in us. Below is another world—the Earth we left behind and must reenter. In the Sun sphere, what I have spoken of as a transformation of the human being now occurs. Our lower being is transformed into the upper being for the next earthly life; thus the legs become the spirit form of the lower jaw, the arms the spirit form of the upper jaw and cheekbones, and so on. This event in the spiritual world is a marvelous work, compared to which any human work on Earth is insignificant. All that human beings accomplish there in conjunction with the higher spiritual beings is grand and majestic. We work there together on the mystery of being human. This all takes place in the Sun realm in the broader sense.

But there is yet another experience for human beings in this realm. If our soul and spirit are *healthy* during earthly life, we must inevitably get a feeling that another world exists, a spiritual world, though we cannot penetrate it with our knowledge. We take the existence of a spiritual world for granted and say that there is a suprasensory world beyond that experienced through our senses.[5] During our existence in the Sun sphere between death and a new birth, however, the situation is reversed. Our experience there is such that we speak of a "world beyond"; here, however, it is the *Earth* that is beyond. It is an intensely alive feeling that awakens in us—not so much concerning one's personal destiny but for the whole essential nature of the Earth.

There is one such characteristic that you can observe and test for yourselves. You should try it, though people today will find it difficult. When you study history and follow it back through the centuries, you can always have a certain kind of experience. You are alive now, in our own time. Go back through history—through the world war to earlier and earlier events until, finally, you arrive at a historical period, back to, let's say, about 1500 or 1550. It begins to feel familiar to you. Consider for a moment such intimate human knowledge; something that lies far in the past seems familiar. You think that this must be something you experienced yourself. Superficial people immediately conclude that this was the period of a previous earthly incarnation. Usually, however, this is not the case. Usually, it is instead the time between death and rebirth in the Sun sphere when you experienced most vividly a connection with earthly existence. It was the

---

5. Rudolf Steiner always speaks of such feelings in relation to a *healthy* soul and spirit: "Certainly there are those who believe quite honestly that the dissolution of the physical body annihilates the soul; and they lead their lives accordingly. It is not necessarily true, however, that these people are completely unbiased in their feelings about such thoughts. Yet, they do not allow their fear of the soul's annihilation and their desire for its continuation to overshadow their reasoning. To that extent, their ideas are often more objective than those whose unconscious belief in the soul's continuing life is based upon a veiled, burning desire for that continuation. Still, the level of prejudice among the deniers of immortality is not less than it is among believers; it is only different" (*A Way of Self-Knowledge*, pp. 106–107).

year when the earthly life presented itself to you in the Sun existence as a "beyond," just as the opposite happens on Earth, where suprasensory life presents itself to you as "beyond."

Let's pause for a moment in considering our path of development after death. We saw that, once we have moved away from the Earth, we complete the Moon existence first. Then we enter the spheres of Mercury, Venus, and Sun, and we continue on from there. Later, we will speak of what follows. None of these events in the spiritual world are isolated; they are also connected to events on Earth. And this leads to a very special relationship. Moon existence is thoroughly permeated with the great primordial teachers of humanity, who we have often mentioned. In very remote antiquity, they left Earth and went into the cosmos to form a cosmic community on the Moon. But there were various people who had been initiated into the Mysteries and later retained a truly living inner vision and hearing of the knowledge that had existed on Earth as the result of those primordial initiates. Consequently, in the Mysteries of the ancient Indian period of civilization, there was still a living knowledge of the Moon initiates' wisdom.[6] This is where we must look for the source of what we can still marvel at today as the echoes of ancient Indian wisdom.

Nor is this all; a twofold event took place. During various later eras, people also felt the influence of the suprasensory realm through which we wander between death and rebirth, though it gradually changed and lessened with each era; in other words, people became less aware of it. The influence that Mercury exerted, for example, was especially strong during the ancient Persian period, but people were less aware of it. Because of this,

6. The whole span of cosmic evolution is described in *An Outline of Esoteric Science*, "Cosmic Evolution and the Human Being"; on the "post-Atlantean civilization of ancient India," see pp. 252–258.

they developed the myth of Ahura Mazda, which was a dim cognition of Mercury's influence on Earth. During the Egypto-
Chaldean era, the active influences were mainly those of Venus.

Then came the wonderful era of Greek culture, which continued in that of the Romans. It was during this Graeco-Latin culture that the Sun influences affected Earth most strongly from the
spiritual world. But humanity was the least aware of such influences during the Graeco-Latin period. This was also when two
things came together. First, during our existence between death
and a new birth when we enter the Sun sphere, we feel an intense
longing to sense the Earth from the Sun. On the other hand,
everything related to the Sun and its nature had a strong influence
on the Greeks. All the Sun forces given to Earth had deep significance for them, especially those known as Athenians (in contrast
to the Spartans). Yet, everything related to the Sun, including its
spiritual aspect, exerted a remarkably deep cosmic influence on
Greece and the whole configuration of the Greek civilization.

Throughout this phase of evolution there was an especially
strong capacity on Earth to perceive the purely spiritual nature of
the starry heavens. Our material perception of the heavens did
not really begin until our fifth post-Atlantean period, which
began in the fifteenth century and is thus only a few hundred
years old. We have, however, already gone past the region where
earthly human beings sense a relationship to the influences they
feel between death and a new birth within the Sun existence.

Today we sense something else much more. Indeed, after the
period in the Sun, we enter the realm of the Mars existence. The
strongest cosmic influence exerted on humanity today is that of
the Mars existence. And we come to know those influences after
experiencing the "noonday" of our life after death, when we turn
back toward Earth. But this entry to the Mars sphere after death
does not mean that the Sun existence ceases to influence us,
because the Sun extends its sphere of influence over all the rest of

the planetary states as well. This continues, but the Mars existence becomes significant for what is now happening on Earth. I will speak more of our journey through Mars existence, but for now I want to connect what we have learned of the spiritual world with what we find specifically active in our own fifth post-Atlantean age.

We are now becoming acquainted with the nature of cosmic battle; we sense it. Most people cannot unravel its mysteries, but a war is being waged in the cosmos between all sorts of good and evil spirits. What we have called the Sun existence assumes special significance for our age. It is very difficult today for spiritual understanding to hold its own against conventional scientific materialism. People are proud of having investigated the Sun from a physical perspective. The Sun is described in scientific books, but such descriptions are unable to convey correct concepts of the Sun. In particular, how does the Sun work in relation to the Earth today? I will point out only one of its activities. It might seem now that I am descending into truly material realms, which may appear strange in contrast to the spiritual events described thus far. What I have to say, however, is important to the progress of our studies.

Of course, you are familiar with a phenomenon called sunspots, which appear with a certain regularity.[7] These are dark spots that appear on the Sun. Sunspots and their meaning have caused much dispute in materialistic science. But if we were to examine them more exactly, we would find that the Sun is inwardly prompted to eject "sun substance" into space through

---

7. Conventional science describes sunspots as dark, usually irregularly shaped spots on the Sun's surface and considered to be solar, magnetic storms. The temperature of the spots is lower than that of the surrounding photosphere; thus the spots are, by contrast, darker. All but the smallest show a dark central portion (the umbra) with a lighter outer area (the penumbra). Sunspot activity peaks every eleven years.

these dark openings. And the substance that is cast out appears in our solar system as comets, meteors, and shooting stars.

Particularly during our age, those beings who rule the universe from within the Sun cast out comets, meteors, and shooting stars. They did so in earlier times as well, but now this activity has a new significance. That is why I said that during earlier times it was mainly the spiritual impulses emanating from the star system that worked. Now, the forces contained in the iron cast out of the Sun begin to have a special significance for human beings. These impulses are used by the spiritual being we call *Michael*, who serves the spirit in the cosmos. So something not present before to this degree has appeared in the cosmos during our time; cosmic iron, with its spiritual significance, makes it possible for Michael to mediate between the suprasensory and the sense-perceptible earthly phenomena.

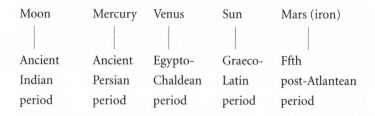

Moon	Mercury	Venus	Sun	Mars (iron)
Ancient Indian period	Ancient Persian period	Egypto- Chaldean period	Graeco- Latin period	Ffth post-Atlantean period

Consequently, in our time we encounter something of a warlike spirit in the world we enter when we go beyond physical existence. In our epoch, when we attain suprasensory insight, cross the threshold, and, rather than concentrating on personal matters, focus on the larger cosmic concerns underlying our whole civilization, we gaze into that other world and perceive battle, strife, and spiritual warfare there. Strife, war, and conflict are behind the scenes of existence in the spiritual realm. What the Sun spirits eject into space as iron in a form that becomes physical also becomes, in the broadest sense, Michael's armor as he accomplishes his task in the cosmic battle to help humanity progress in the face of strife and war, the forces behind the scenes of today's civilization. On the one hand, there is war and strife, on the other, the work of Michael.[8]

Again, this all relates to the development of human freedom. As you can see, as earthly human beings our blood contains iron. Even if we had no iron in our blood, the impulse and feeling for freedom would still arise in our souls, but our bodies would be unable to act on that impulse. Because we can learn how Michael is able to use cosmic iron (which was also cast out in former times), we can not only understand the concept of freedom and its impulse, but we can also sense the *body's* power to carry the impulse of freedom. By understanding the Michael impulse correctly, we can learn how to use the iron within us for spiritual freedom.

External matter has meaning to us only when we understand it as an expression of spirit in the world. In our age, we must learn to use the iron in our blood properly. Wherever there is iron, there is also a cosmic or human impulse to develop freedom. It was out of deep, inherent knowledge that the ancient initiates ascribed iron to Mars; with its importance for human blood, iron also has importance for the cosmos.

We can understand these things today through a renewed spiritual science. It is not a matter of reviving ancient traditions but one of rediscovery through spiritual science itself. When anthroposophy happens to agree with ancient lore, it does not mean that anthroposophy merely revives what is old. Anthroposophy investigates and studies matters in terms of their own essential nature. These things regain their meaning when we see how such knowledge once belonged to human beings through the influence of the

---

8. See "The Michael Letters" in *Anthroposophical Leading Thoughts*, Rudolf Steiner Press, London, 1998.

primordial, divine wisdom of the beings who left Earth for the Moon, and who live today in the community of the Moon.

And so, our age is also connected with what we experience between death and rebirth. Therefore, the perception of earthly occurrences is strongest while we are in the Sun sphere, though it is always present to some degree after we die; between death and a new birth, we continually look back to the earthly realm from the supraearthly regions. If we did not, the earthly realm would become alien to us during our long journey between death and rebirth.

Human experiences in the suprasensory world can be described in a myriad of ways. Yesterday I described them to you one way, and now I have described them to you in relation to the starry world and in connection with what takes place on Earth during successive human cultures. All of these things must be brought gradually into a whole. No one should come and say "One time he described our passage through the period between death and rebirth one way, and then another time he described it very differently." If you go to a city once, twice, or even three times, you will certainly describe things differently according to what you learn about the city each time. Eventually, you must bring all the details of your descriptions together. Similarly, the descriptions of human experiences in the suprasensory world must be brought together, and then looked at and pondered together. Only then can we get an impression of the real nature of the suprasensory world and what we experience there.

That is as far as I wanted to go for now. In today's second lecture I will continue from here and describe our further experiences between death and new birth.

4. Through Midnight to Birth

evening, NOVEMBER, 17, 1923

IN THE LECTURE earlier today, we looked at how our life between death and a new birth can be conceived of as a journey through spheres of the spiritual world. We saw at the same time how one can gain a perspective for this journey through certain spiritual regions in reference to the positions of specific stars. But before going further, let us look more closely at the nature of this passage through such areas marked by positions of stars.

It might seem as though it would be enough to describe suprasensory human existence between two earthly lives only as it was presented in *Theosophy*, for instance. Certainly, it is absolutely right to begin by becoming familiar with those realms in this way. But our knowledge must progress and expand. Thus it is necessary to approach these matters in a way that includes the unity of the cosmos and the harmonious cooperation between the suprasensory and sensory worlds. And it may be said in this connection that the whole relationship of the various regions traversed between death and a new birth is also manifested in terms of spatio-temporal relationships between the stars. Therefore, we present a true picture by speaking of these spiritual regions in terms related to the stars. And it is true indeed that when pointing to a star we indicate a place to which we must refer in relation to any suprasensory region.

It could be argued that what exists between death and a new birth cannot be thought of in terms of space—or perhaps only to a certain degree. This is perfectly true, but it does have something to do with space. *Everything* outside space and time plays into space and time, and because people must think and conceptualize in spatio-temporal terms, the imagery of the stars, once acquired, provides an excellent image of what lies beyond the senses.

One thing, however, must be added. We learn in physics that processes in the physical world that are subject to gravity change out in cosmic space. Physicists report that gravity decreases in proportion to the square of the distance. The intensity of light also ebbs in the same proportion. But people refuse to admit one thing—that all knowledge derived from Earth about physical matters (such as gravity, light, and so on) is from this Earth, and though it applies to Earth and its immediate environment, it is plausible that it very well might lose some degree of validity out in space. We are thus justified in speaking of today's generally-accepted knowledge as true only for Earth and its immediate surroundings.

Just as gravitational force decreases in proportion to the square of the distance, so, too, the truth of our conclusions decreases as we move away from Earth. When an astronomer or astrophysicist, for example, uses ordinary thinking to determine what takes place in a spiral nebula out in space, it is like trying to calculate the weight of a stone, according to conditions on Earth, in a spiral nebula way out in the heavens. Consequently, we should not be surprised when spiritual science tells us that matters look one way here on Earth, and completely different out in the cosmos. Here, the Moon appears as we are used to seeing it, but in reality it is a cosmic community consisting of what I described in this afternoon's lecture. Those are the facts regarding the stars and constellations. We must keep this in mind as I describe the matters that now become the object of our studies.

So far, the lectures have brought us to the point where we move into the Sun sphere during our life between death and a new birth. In this region, the spirit form of the lower part of the human being changes into what the head will become in the next earthly life. We must remember, of course, that our path between death and a new birth takes us through all these planetary spheres *twice*. After death we pass first into the Moon sphere, then we go on into the spheres of Mercury, Venus, and the Sun. That is where we left off in our description.

In the Sun sphere, the lower human being begins to be transformed into the upper human, so that the limbs are transformed, at first spiritually, into what will be the human head organization. This metamorphosis is an infinitely grand and sublime work. And anyone who studies the human head only in a physical connection has no idea of all that must work together in the cosmos to bring about the spiritual model of this human head—a seed that then unites with the physical embryo. This work on the spiritual model of the head, which then acts upon the physical embryo, begins during the period after death that we spend in the region of the Sun.

After this work has been begun in the Sun sphere, we go into the Mars sphere, then into the Jupiter and Saturn spheres. The Saturn sphere is really the last one that we then enter, since Uranus and Neptune do not enter our picture. During this whole time spent passing through these realms, we work on the spiritual archetype of the head. Our path then leads us even farther into the cosmic expanse, out into the vast cosmic ocean where metamorphosis continues until we begin our return path. Then, returning through the regions of Saturn, Jupiter, and Mars to the region of the Sun, we come again finally to the sphere of the Moon. We will hear more about this return path later; for now we will consider our experiences once our time in the region of the Sun is ended.

Until we reach the Sun sphere, our experiences are connected most closely with ourselves. In the previous lecture I told you about how we wear a countenance that expresses our good and bad qualities and how this enables us to see others who are similar to ourselves. I also told you how we gradually change our spirit form and begin to resemble the beings of the suprasensory world and how we are then able to view the beings of the third and second hierarchies. If we wish to describe human beings up to the stage of the Sun existence, we must focus on and describe their spirit form. But, once we enter the Sun region, we experience something I refer to as *living into cosmic music*, or music of the spheres. We hear the meaning of all the interplay between the starry realms in the cosmic harmony and melody. This interactivity of the stars (which simultaneously expresses the interaction of the spiritual beings in these regions) ultimately evokes the phenomenon expressed as cosmic harmony and cosmic melody.

It is primarily the life of feeling in its spiritual metamorphosis that is quickened and stimulated as we enter the Sun existence. Our whole experience is like cosmic melody and cosmic harmony that vibrates through our whole being. At this stage of our life between death and a new birth, we do not need theory or anything that can be expressed in words. What we need is the *universal feeling* that fills our entire being—the melodious and harmonious quality with which the various cosmic beings work together. And now something else occurs that clearly shows us the relationship of the two worlds—the physical, sensory world and the suprasensory, or extraphysical world. The moment we enter the Sun existence and are approached by the melodies and harmonies of the spheres from every direction of the cosmos, we sense the last remnants of one of the most spiritual faculties we had during earthly existence—the last remnants of speech.

Now, even our spiritual shape has fallen away during our journey between death and rebirth; we have become like the round sphere of the universe, because our human form has been transformed into a head shape during our Sun existence. In other words, everything about our spirit form that could remind us of earthly existence has fallen away. Now the aspect of our earthly being that was expressed through our ability to speak and pour thoughts into the form of words—the soul meaning of our speech—crops up uncomfortably (at least, as things are at present on Earth) in the memory as a dissonant element in the cosmic music. A dissonant element actually enters the cosmic music, because we carry a remnant of our speech capacities into our Sun sphere existence. What we carry into this sphere becomes the basis for the work of certain higher beings whose task is to help the Earth from their place in the cosmos. Above all, they see in human speech how earthly existence has decayed and degenerated.

Human speech does not really develop out of us with elemental force in any of the current European or American languages. Perhaps the nature of what speech was at one time could manifest again on Earth owing to the fact that some of us are learning eurythmy. What really happens when we learn eurythmy? Today a word is spoken casually, without the slightest idea of how its whole structure is related to our inner soul experience. Indeed, the way words are spoken today merely conforms to convention. People no longer give thought to the fact that by saying "ah" as a separate sound, they express the pure sound of the soul's awe and wonder. By speaking the sound b, we imply that something is being covered, enveloped, or wrapped up. Consonants invariably refer to *forms*; vowels always signify *feeling*. The inner essence of soul is represented by vowels, and form always by consonants. Consequently, b is primordially connected with enfolding; it is really a dwelling, so to speak, or little house. When I speak the sound of b, I signify enfolding. When I say "ah," it expresses wonder in the very depths of my soul. The consonant sound of t expresses settling down, stopping and lingering. The sound of d is a gentler stop.

Suppose I say *"Bad"* [German for *bath*]. If I go back to the word's origin, when it was truly felt and seen, I would say, "The water surrounds me as an enveloping sheath"—*b*. "It is comfortably warm"—*ah*. I am led to *ah*, and now "I stay within it"—*d*. This whole experience is contained in the word. Today, this kind of analysis is somewhat humorous, because people no longer experience words. If we wanted to experience the word *B-a-d* we would say, "This dwelling, where I feel wonder and in which I sit." Speech is indeed filled with soul experience; the inner experience of the human soul flows into and permeates it. Speech was once such that one could sense it in this way.

In the original, primordial languages, speech was all perception of feeling and form—the perception of feeling in vowels and form in consonants. Today this has fallen away, leaving only convention. Our way of life is such that words have become no more than memorized habit. In eurythmy, however, we transform the sounds *b-a-d* back into their corresponding gestures. In performing the gestures, a eurythmist must reclaim the *experience* of speech. One may hope that, as more and more people come to love eurythmy, people will find their way back to a way of speaking that is felt and seen; this was the nature of the primordial tongues. In this way, eurythmy will eventually become much more than the new art it is now. It will become a guide to show human beings how the spiritual soul life may be carried on the waves and rhythms of speech. Now is a time when many people speak with such little articulation (let alone, *soul*) that we can no longer really call it "speech" at all. People "spit" their words. In speech today very little is born from the soul. There is real cause for despair in today's lack of soul and life in words, not to mention the failure even to articulate.

So, in our day, when human beings enter the Sun existence after death, a shrill discord arises from Earth into the music of the cosmos. And it is precisely this condition of speech that helps certain spiritual beings to recognize degenerate manifestations in earthly existence, and how to find the forces and impulses that can return to a kind of ascent.

We continue our journey between death and a new birth and, thus, enter the Mars existence. What does it mean to say that we enter Mars existence? At this point we can no longer speak of a human spirit *form*, because now the human being has been completely transformed into a spiritual image of the great cosmic spheres. The path leads on and on, through the spheres of Mars, Jupiter, Saturn, and into billowing waves of the cosmos. In the region of Mars, human beings experience the "population" of Mars. These inhabitants of Mars are revealed as either discarnate human souls or hierarchical beings, mostly those of the higher hierarchies from whose entire being *cosmic speech* reverberates into space. Human beings have now arrived in the region where cosmic music becomes cosmic speech. At first they hear it, and then they become interwoven with cosmic speech themselves. Instead of the *imitative* human speech, they listen to *creative* speech, speech through which things come into being. This takes place during our passage through the Mars sphere.

While we pass through the Mars sphere, we learn in a conscious way from the beings there. The spiritual population of the Mars sphere consists of beings who *know* the cosmic speech, along with other beings who are warlike, and so on. But, human beings are concerned primarily with the beings of the Mars sphere who are in fact wholly cosmic word. These are the protectors of cosmic speech.

Our journey then leads us into the region of Jupiter, where beings guard *cosmic thought*. These beings radiate thought entities into our planetary system and its environs. And now we pass through this region, in which we become involved in a metamorphosis that I can describe only in the following, rather schematic way.

Picture how human beings become a kind of image of the cosmic spheres, into a spirit model for the head of their next earthly incarnation. After we have learned from the shrill dissonance of the earthly speech in the Sun existence to lay aside this earthly speech, we grow into the cosmic speech while passing through Mars. We receive there the first predisposition for understanding cosmic speech. After the described transformation has begun, metamorphosing our lower limbs, the legs, into the lower jaw, the arms into the upper jaw, and so on, we work at first with the beings of the higher hierarchies preparing the spiritual model of the head. But during this time, the head is being prepared to understand the cosmos, not the Earth. And it first learns cosmic speech and cosmic thoughts. Cosmic thoughts and cosmic speech live into human heads there. And just as here on Earth we know something about the mineral, plant, and animal kingdoms, so, on our journeying through Mars and Jupiter, do we know the mysteries of the spiritual cosmos. We develop the right feeling for what it is to be a human being when we become aware that as we pass through life between death and a new birth we learn all the names of the wonderful, majestic beings of the higher hierarchies, learn to understand what creative functions they perform in the universe, to form judgments not about how to get from The Hague to Amsterdam but about how cosmic epoch emerges from cosmic epoch through the creative activity of the higher hierarchies. Such is the transit through Jupiter.

Next we pass through Saturn existence. Saturn endows us with what we could call *cosmic memory*. Saturn is the cosmic region of spiritual beings who preserve the memory of all that has ever happened in our planetary system. Saturn is the grand repository of memories of all planetary events. In the Mars sphere, we learned the speech of the gods, and in the Jupiter sphere the thoughts of the gods; now, in our first transit through Saturn existence, we learn everything the gods of our planetary system remember.

Thus, there is built into the spiritual archetype of our future earthly heads all that will prepare us to be citizens of the cosmos and to live among beings of the hierarchies, just as we live on Earth among the subordinate kingdoms of minerals, plants, and animals.

Then, once we have been enriched deeply in our spiritual existence to the degree that we understand the speech of the macrocosm (in the broadest sense of the word), we enter the region called the sphere of fixed stars. In this region there is no longer planetary activity, but the activity of fixed stars. There, work is done in the most profound sense for the first time, with the cooperation of endless spiritual worlds, to bring together the elements needed for the primal archetype of the human head.

Then we begin our return path, first into the Saturn sphere (which we can talk about tomorrow). Because we received the planetary memory into ourselves during our earlier transit through the Saturn sphere, a basis can now be established in the head for the faculty of memory needed in earthly life. Cosmic memory implanted into our being and made "earthly"; it is transformed into the capacity of human memory. And in the Jupiter sphere on the return path, all that we acquired by perceiving the thoughts of the gods becomes our capacity for understanding human thoughts reflected by ordinary consciousness once the spiritual archetype of the head has joined with the archetype of the physical embryo.

Now, however, during our return through Saturn, a detailed plan can take place for the metamorphosis of the lower human into the various parts of the head. This is a wonderful activity— one human being works on another in harmony with the beings of the higher hierarchies. Truly, the work accomplished here in forming the human head is not unlike creating a whole universe. In the sphere I am now speaking of as the existence between death and rebirth, every individual human head is seen as a wonderful world, one of infinite variety and detail. And this work requires the devotion of human beings linked by destiny, along with the cooperation and necessary effort of hierarchical beings who understand, out of the mysteries of the cosmos, how to form the human head.

It is indeed wonderful to learn in this way about how we are constituted as human beings. Such knowledge cannot lead to pride or conceit; the world in which we live between death and a new birth prevents us from developing conceit. It would be absurd to fall prey to human delusions of grandeur among beings of the hierarchies—the seraphim, cherubim, and thrones—because we always remain small compared to those beings with whom we create. In earthly existence, when we discover our nature in relation to the grand cosmic macrocosm between death and a new birth, we have good reason to remind ourselves of how little we really brought with us into earthly existence. We have very little cause to be proud of our present condition; nor can we be very proud of the way we were among the gods. By seeing what happens to us between death and a new birth, we can assess the true meaning of our humanity according to the work of the gods on us between death and rebirth, and we can gain a real sense of our responsibility and the tremendous effort we need to make to be worthy of our human status on Earth.

Now, along our path of return, we reenter the Mars existence as the work on our being continues. The spiritual archetype for the structure of a new body is added—the chest and limb organizations for our next earthly life. It is indeed true that the basis for the limbs in the previous earthly life now emerge as the basis for the head in the next incarnation; during our journey through the starry world on the way to the next earthly life, new seeds are generated for the chest and limbs. The nature of this preparation is, of course, spiritual.

As we pass through Mars again, what we acquired as the most sublime spirituality during our first passage through Mars that gave us the capacity to understand the cosmic word, now becomes somewhat lower spiritually. It is transformed into a spiritual substance that later becomes the human I-being. Also, during our return through this sphere, the spiritual archetype for the larynx and respiratory system is added.

Then we come again to the Sun existence. This second journey through the Sun sphere is extremely significant. Since our first sojourn in the Sun existence, we passed through the spheres of Mars, Jupiter, and Saturn into the realm of the stars, and now we return through Saturn, Jupiter, and Mars. During this whole time, our entire being has been surrendered to and united with the cosmos. We have lived in the cosmos and learned cosmic speech; we have learned to weave cosmic thoughts into our being. We have not lived in our own memory (which comes to life later for us) but in the memory of the whole planetary system. We have felt united with the beings of the higher hierarchies in the memory of cosmic thoughts and cosmic speech. Now we return to the Sun existence, where we begin to withdraw again to become separate, individual beings. There is a vague, dawning feeling of separating from the cosmos. This is because the archetype for the human heart is now being established within us.

The return journey continues as we pass through the Venus and Mercury spheres for the second time. There the spiritual archetypes of the remaining organs are planted within us. After our second transit through the Sun sphere (and such transits can span long periods of time), and well before we reenter earthly existence, a highly significant turn of events takes place. On our return journey to Earth through the cosmos, we prepare the spiritual seed of the heart. This heart is not, of course, merely the form for a physical heart, though it has been indicated; it is a form enveloped by and interwoven with our entire worth as individual human beings as a result of prior earthly lives. The most important thing is not that we receive the archetype of the physical heart into ourselves in the Sun sphere, but that this heart seed concentrates our whole moral being—our qualities of soul and spirit. This is all concentrated in the human heart.

Prior to the uniting of the archetypal heart with the embryonic foundation of the future body, the cosmic heart is a spiritual and moral soul entity within us. We then unite this spiritual and moral soul essence, which we acquire and experience as we return to Earth, with the archetype of the embryo. This concentration of our spiritual and moral soul nature is experienced by us in concert with the sublime beings of the Sun, who oversee the creative forces of the whole planetary system and, consequently, our existence on the Earth.

Allow me to use an image to describe this to you. The expressions may sound strange, but they are appropriate. When we are given this cosmic heart, we are surrounded by the spiritual beings of the hierarchies who direct the whole planetary system in relation to earthly existence. Here our attention is drawn to something absolutely magnificent and marvelous. It is difficult to describe what the human being experienced during this phase. In a certain sense, it is not unlike the way we feel in physical existence. In physical existence we feel intimately connected with our heartbeat and the heart's activity as a whole; likewise, through our microcosmic spiritual heart we feel united with our whole being of soul and spirit. The moral being of soul and spirit that we have become at this moment of experience is a "spiritual heartbeat" within us. Our whole being thus seems to be in the cosmos, just as our heartbeat is in us. We sense our whole being in the cosmos like our own heartbeat, and we feel a kind of circulatory process connected with it.

On Earth, we feel the blood's circulation in our heartbeat and our breathing in relation to it; similarly, on our return journey through the Sun existence (if I may express it in such an image) we feel the beat of our spiritual, macrocosmic heart, and we feel as though currents were flowing from there to beings of the second hierarchy. Just as in the physical organism our blood flows to the heart from the veins, likewise, the words of exusiai, kyriotetes, and dynamis pour into our spiritual soul being (now located within us) all that they say about the cosmos and cosmic judgment of human beings. The spirit of the cosmos, its words, and its tones become the circulation concentrated in this spiritual macrocosmic beating heart, the spiritual and moral soul of the human being. It is our spiritual human heart beating.

At the same time, however, it is also the heartbeat of the world itself, the world we are in. And there the works and forces that flow from the creative beings of the second hierarchy are experienced as the bloodstream. The human bloodstream is concentrated in the heart so that we can sense it subconsciously; the heart is indeed a sense organ for perceiving the blood's movement, not a pump as physicists claim; the coursing of blood is brought about by our spirituality and vitality. Likewise, during this period of our life between death and a new birth, we are graciously privileged to bear within us one of these perceptive organs, a cosmic heart created from the macrocosmic pulse that springs from the activity of the second hierarchy.

Our return journey continues through the spheres of Mercury and Venus. First however, at the cosmic moment when we may truly sense that we are within the spiritual, cosmic heart, we view the lineage of generations, ending with the parents to whom we will be born. Thus we are connected with our ancestral line relatively early. We are born of a father and a mother, who each have a father and a mother, and so on, looking back about a hundred years. But we must go even farther back, through several more centuries, because long before our birth on Earth, we will have united with the genetic line that culminates with our next family.

We determine our connection with that family line very early, while passing through the Sun existence I have described. In our transit through the cosmic communities of Venus and Mercury we are able to determine, somewhat, our destiny so that it aligns as closely as possible with the circumstantial conditions we must experience through birth within a particular family and nation.

Then we reenter the Moon sphere. Please recall that during our first transit through the Moon sphere our thoughts were directed toward the primordial sages and to Earth—in terms of both evil and good—back to the beginning of Earth's existence when suprahuman teachers imparted superior wisdom to earthly human beings. Now as we enter the Moon existence for the second time, our attention is drawn less toward ancient earthly events. The time we spend in this cosmic Moon existence corresponds to the time between earthly conception and birth; thus, the life of the human embryo is accompanied by a certain cosmic development. In the Moon sphere, we pass through a certain phase of evolution, while on Earth there is a step-by-step preparation of the physical embryo with which we gradually unite.

And what are we doing in a macrocosmic sense during this second Moon development? In all of the experiences I have described thus far, human consciousness is much more clear and awake than ordinary consciousness during earthly life. It is tremendously important to be perfectly clear about the fact that dreaming consciousness is dull and waking consciousness is bright, and that our consciousness after death is even brighter. Our whole life here on Earth is dreamy compared to the brightness of our awareness after death. Furthermore, with each new stage of life after death, consciousness becomes clearer and more alert.

When we first ascend through the Moon sphere, our consciousness brightens because we enter the environment of the wise, primordial teachers of humanity. On our passage through the Mercury and Venus spheres, it grows brighter still. It thus becomes brighter with every entrance to another starry realm. During our return earthward, however, our consciousness goes through a corresponding, sphere-by-sphere dimming, although as we reach Mercury it is still brighter than in ordinary, earthly life. But then we enter the Moon region. In this environment, we are shown what we were as human beings at the beginning of earthly evolution. Our consciousness is extinguished when we return to that sphere. There we experienced the first illumined view of the suprasensory world in a state of consciousness brighter than any we can have on Earth, and, on the return to Earth our consciousness is dimmed to the point where it serves as no more than the forces of growth in a dreamy, little child; our consciousness has dimmed to a dreamy quality. Only then is it possible to unite what we have developed as our spiritual soul being with the embryo. Because of the single fact that we can have this necessary connection with the physical embryo, we develop in the Moon sphere in the company of the primordial teachers of humanity for a period that parallels the ten lunar months of embryonic development in the mother's body. This Moon development involves the cooperation of an entire community of those teachers in reducing the consciousness we possessed on Mercury to the dreamy level of our reentry to earthly existence.

We can understand the physical human being we see here on Earth only through insight into the suprasensory nature of the human being. Our suprasensory being can never be comprehended through earthly information, but only through spiritual knowledge of the macrocosm. Thus far, our lectures were intended to show how we, as earthly beings, must be born from the cosmos as *spiritual* human beings.

In tomorrow's lecture we will look at the significance of earthly life itself, inasmuch as this suprahuman being enters earthly life.

And we will come to understand why we leave it again and pass through the gate of death, taking into the spiritual world all that we acquire during our life here. Now that we have become acquainted with some aspects of our spiritual, suprasensory being, tomorrow we shall return and consider the relationship between the suprasensory and physical human being.

5. Earth and the Mystery of Karma

NOVEMBER 18, 1923

TO THE BEST of our ability, we have tried in a few short hours to look at the human journey through the suprasensory world, the realm where human beings live between death and a new birth. Although we are usually unaware of it, our human forces also reach into that world while we are here on the physical Earth in our physical and etheric bodies. In the physical world we sense our suprasensory existence more or less as mystery—one that, unless we find at least a partial answer to it, leaves us inwardly without harmony, stability, and security. Indeed, our very life would lack energy and vitality, and true human love would remain beyond reach.

Just by observing the human being here, we can see an aspect of our suprasensory human nature, and this can help us understand why the divine spiritual realms sent us into this world of physical senses. In fact, the reason is that knowledge of the suprasensory world must first be spoken of to people here in the physical world. We would have to approach questions of the suprasensory world very differently if we were to speak of them to those who have died and who are passing through their existence between death and a new birth. So today, as we consider human life on Earth, it will be appropriate to conclude our study by allowing our minds to light up with what we have received so far concerning the mysteries of the suprasensory world.

Let us begin by considering human life on Earth—in other words, let us consider ourselves. First, we have our senses; they provide us with information about all that surrounds us. Our senses are the cause of our earthly joy and happiness as well as our suffering and pain. As human beings, we sometimes fail to consider how significant our sense impressions and experiences are for our lives. And studies such as we have been devoting ourselves to for the past several days take us beyond our life of the senses into spiritual realms. It might seem as though this anthroposophic spiritual science could lead us to underrate sensory life, even to the point of saying that it has little importance and that we should escape it in our own earthly life. Such an attitude, however, is not the result of a spiritual scientific study. Such feelings can never be the *ultimate* goal of spiritual science. It simply tells us that there are certain ways of living life in the senses that are incompatible with human worth and dignity, and that it is possible to give up the life of the senses in its inferior aspects and regain its deeper significance on a higher, spiritual level. We would have good reason to avoid spiritual study if it took away the meaning of all the beauty that flows into our souls when we observe the wonderful world of flowering plants and fruiting trees or any other aspect of the natural realm, such as the starry heavens and so on, and if, as a result, we were advised to abandon all this in favor of spiritual contemplation. But this is not at all how it is.

When you recall what the initiates and masters of various ages offered for the perfection and dignity of human life, you find that they never diminished the beauty, splendor, and majesty of our earthly life of the senses. Their poetry and other arts were marvelous when describing suprasensory reality. We have only to recall such images as the lotus flower to see that initiates never shied from depicting the spiritual development through images grounded in sensory experience, and that it was their belief that what we find—or at least *can* find—in the world of the senses leads to the highest.

But we human beings cannot find satisfaction in the sensory world as perceived by ordinary consciousness, because, although the impressions that enter us through our eyes and ears and other senses is connected with our I-being and its whole life and development, it does not really give our I anything to support inner certainty. We gaze outward to the beauty and splendor of flowers and face a world of infinite variety. When we turn our gaze inward, toward the I, at first our ordinary consciousness feels as though the I has vanished. It seems like it is merely a point of spirit within us that says little more than the empty word *I*. This is also not surprising. Just consider that before the eye can see it must forget itself completely. It is the nature of our senses that they must surrender to the world so that they can mediate properly between the world and the human being. The eye has to be completely transparent to convey the glory, grandeur, and beauty of the outer world in all its brilliant color and radiance, and the same is true of the other senses.

Really, we know nothing of our senses. Is there any way we can know and understand their true nature? To do this we must again follow the path to the suprasensory world. Even knowledge of the senses is gained only by traversing the suprasensory world.

You are all familiar with my descriptions of the paths that lead into the higher worlds.[1] Try to picture vividly what *imaginative* knowledge can be. You withdraw from physical perception of the outer world and enter *imaginative* cognition. But the most interesting thing that happens on this path is something I will describe

---

1. See, for example, *A Way of Self-Knowledge* and *How to Know Higher Worlds*.

for you through an image. When you approach the world of *imagination* in meditation (using methods presented in some familiar book on the subject), you begin to struggle to free the etheric body from your physical organism, so that this etheric body (our first suprasensory aspect) becomes conscious to some degree. You can detect the point in time when you are between ordinary sensory perception and *imaginative* perception—when you have not yet attained *imagination* in a developed sense, but are on the way to it.

Now let us picture a person who is on the way from ordinary sensory perception to *imagination* and is traveling into high mountains where granite is especially abundant—granite with a high content of quartz or silica. As we work toward *imagination*, our soul forces can develop especially well amid an abundance of silicious rock that is rich in quartz. We succeed in developing certain inner soul capacities on the first attempt, because high mountain quartz rock makes a special impression on us. This quartz is initially only slightly transparent. But as soon as we have struggled through to the stage I have described, this mineral becomes completely transparent. We climb into the high mountains, and the siliceous rock appears as transparent as glass, but in such a way that one has the feeling that something flows from one's own being to unite with the siliceous rock.

Right there, at the Earth's outermost surface, through a kind of natural offering of our consciousness, we unite with the Earth's whole surface. At this moment it seems as though our very eyes are sending out streams that penetrate the quartz; at the same moment something comes to life in us that causes us to feel united with the whole Earth's existence. In this unity with the quartz—feeling one with the whole universe—we experience our first real oneness with it that is not merely the product of a dream or some abstract thought. In this way, an intimate awareness can light up within us, which perhaps I can express by saying, "Earth, you are not alone in the cosmos; you are indeed one with the great cosmos, along with me and all earthly beings." Through this experience of oneness with the siliceous rock, we no longer view the Earth as separate from the rest of the universe, but as one etheric sphere formed from the universal etheric sphere.

This is our first feeling. There are many ancient songs and ancient myths filled with wondrous revelations that sing to us across the ages in the literature from a time of inherent human clairvoyance. Today, people read such songs and myths and like to feel that it lifts their hearts and souls. But the truth of such songs and myths eludes people of our time. We cannot even be affected by a true feeling for the Bhagavad Gita, for example, or some other Indian or Eastern literature, unless spiritual insight shows us the real possibility of our unity with the Earth, leading to oneness with the whole cosmos. In many cases, the mood of those old songs and ballads arose from such oneness. It is like a "walking in consciousness" with light, a light that penetrates the hard quartz, making it a cosmic eye through which we can look out into the vast expanses of the universe.

Indeed, we can say that when we begin from reality in our description of the suprasensory human being, we feel inherently disinclined to be abstract and theoretical. Rather, we are predisposed to present it in a way that links the feeling life of the human soul to the ideas we express. This should deeply stir our hearts whenever we study our suprasensory nature—that it is impossible to express our spiritual knowledge without uniting our thoughts and ideas with the whole human being in will and feeling. We must endure life, but one of the things most difficult to bear for those who are aware of the true human elements of suprasensory knowledge is to hear the way certain people turn spiritual understanding into fixed theories. Theoretical discussion of the spiritual world is no less painful than holding your finger in a flame.

After we have progressed a certain degree in suprasensory cognition—when we understand through *imagination* the suprasensory forces that are active in us between birth and death—we can continue by attaining the level of suprasensory knowledge related to *inspiration*. Through *inspiration*, we can see into the nature of what we were before birth when we descended into earthly life, and we can also see what we will become after passing through the gate of death. Everything described in these lectures can be seen—our journey through the various regions in which our countenance is formed and where we metamorphose from the previous life into a new earthly life. Through *inspiration*, we can view everything I have described as our journey through the various starry worlds.

Inspiration, through which we look so deeply into our own inner being, assumes a particular nuance when we consider that what can be described as our experience in the life between death and rebirth also lives in us during our life here on Earth. Indeed, all the grandeur and cosmic majesty that must be portrayed by describing the true human being as a denizen of the starry worlds—and indeed even the worlds of the higher hierarchies— is also alive in us as we stand here on the Earth, seemingly insignificant creatures from the spatial perspective within the skin of our physical bodies. Inasmuch as our knowledge can penetrate what we contain as a physical heritage of our true being between death and a new birth, we can also do something more; we can penetrate to the depths of our planet Earth, to its veins of metal ores of lead, silver, and copper, to everything that lives as the metallic elements of the rocky Earth. When observed with the ordinary senses, the metallic substances initially do little more than suggest the various kinds of earth in which they occur. But when we penetrate the Earth with the spiritually honed perception that tells us about the human spirit, something special happens to the metallic elements within the Earth. All the copper, silver, and gold in the earth begin to speak in a rich and mysterious language. As we live on Earth, we are confronted by something that gives us a more intimate relationship with the living soul being of the Earth itself. Metal ores tell us something—they become cosmic memories for us. This is actually what happens. Consider yourselves, for example. When you nurture an active, inner stillness and allow old memories to bring many things into your soul, you feel as though you were living again in numerous past experiences. You reconnect with many who, over the course of your life, became dear and may have died long ago. You feel remote from the present and deeply involved with the joys and sorrows of previous experiences you have lived through.

Something very similar, but on a much larger scale, happens when we unite with the veins of metal in the earth through the inner light of spiritual insight, of suprasensory cognition. This is different from the experience of quartz, in which we are transported in a kind of visual sense into the vast cosmic expanses. In this case we become one, in a certain sense, with the body of the Earth. As you perceive inwardly the metallic veins in their wonderful speech, you feel united with the innermost soul and heartbeat of the Earth itself, and you become aware of memories that are not your own. Memories echo inwardly; they are the Earth's own memories of its earlier stages, before it was our Earth; before the present animal and plant kingdoms began to dwell on it; and before the minerals that now exist in its depths. Along with the Earth, one remembers those ancient days when the Earth was united with the other planets in our solar system. One recalls ages when the Earth had not yet separated, because it had not yet condensed and become firm within as it is today. One recalls a time when the whole solar system was an ensouled, living organism, and human beings lived within it in a very different form. Thus, the metallic veins in the earth lead us to the Earth's own memories. When we have this inner experience, we can understand very clearly why we are sent to the Earth by the divine spiritual beings who guide the universal order.

Living in the Earth's memories like this causes us to gain a real sense of our own thinking for the first time. Because we have comprehended Earth's memories, we feel how our thinking is connected with the Earth itself. And the moment we make the Earth's memories our own, we are surrounded by the beings of the second hierarchy (kyriotetes, dynamis, and exusiai). This is how, even in earthly life, we may be surrounded by the beings who surround us at a certain time between death and a new birth, as described. We fully realize that we contact beings of the second hierarchy while we are incarnated on Earth between birth and death. But these beings do more than work with us between death and rebirth to transform our being; they also play a role in forming the cosmos as a whole. Here we see how the higher cosmic order gives these beings the responsibility for everything in the Earth related to the influences of those veins of metal.

Now we can look back again. What I discussed before about the experience of quartz was probably not immediately understood, because it is not very obvious. But our marvelous experience of the Earth's memories in relation to the veins of metal *does* speak plainly. Now, however, we can return and try to understand something that perhaps was not understood at first.

Now we become aware that we are surrounded by beings of the third hierarchy (angels, archangels, and archai) as we soar into the great cosmic whole, borne by the light that permeates quartz. And we learn something very special; as we ascend into the high mountains or descend to veins of metal deep in the Earth, the reality of it is not communicated to us by our ordinary senses. We become familiar with the marvel that, in the high mountain regions of the siliceous rock, angels, archangels, and archai weave and hover over those rocky peaks. And when we descend into the

Earth, we find the beings of the second hierarchy permeate the paths of metallic veins. We can also say that during earthly life we are among the spiritual beings connected with our innermost being between death and a new birth.

When a certain time has elapsed after passing through the gate of death, we arrive consciously in the realms of angels, archangels, and archai. The condition of consciousness we have developed in this disembodied state enables us to perceive the beings around us, just as we perceive the four kingdoms of the natural world during our life on Earth. But when our higher level of consciousness there enables us to behold angels, archangels, and archai, everything that the senses could perceive has disappeared, because our senses have been surrendered to the elements with our bodies. Between death and a new birth we perceive nothing of the earthly, sensory life.

Then the angels, archangels, and archai narrate for us the story of what they are doing down on Earth (this is the appropriate way to say it, since it fits the situation exactly). They recount how they are occupied with more than the life they live with us; they whisper, "We also participate in cosmic creation; we are the creative beings of the cosmos, and we look down in Earth existence upon the earthly forms shaped by the quartz rock and its relatives." Then, while among these angels, archangels, and archai between death and new birth, we realize that we must return to Earth, because during this time we come to know the beings of the third hierarchy. We also hear them speak in a wonderful way of their works on Earth. We realize that we can perceive their activities only by descending to Earth, clothed in a physical, human body, and thus partaking of sensory impressions.

Indeed, the deepest secrets of sensory perception—not just those available in high mountain country, but everything that the senses convey—are revealed to us in the wonderful words of

beings we are associated with between death and rebirth. Ordinary consciousness just cannot perceive the real mystery and
beauty of physical nature, which is so great that, after passing
through the gate of death, our earthly memories of it are truly
illuminated when we hear the third hierarchy describe what we
perceived with our eyes, ears, and other senses on Earth.

Thus is the connection between what is physical and supraphysical. It is also the connection between physical human life
and supraphysical life.

The universe is full of splendor, and it is only proper that
everything we see in physical existence delights and uplifts us.
We come to know its actual mysteries once we have passed
through the gate of death. The more we learn to rejoice in the
physical world, the more deeply we enter into all the joy that the
sense world bestows and the greater the measure of understanding that we bring to the realm of the angels. They are waiting to
tell us of the mysteries here on Earth that we cannot yet understand, but that we do understand once we pass into the supraphysical realm.

And our relationship is similar in the case of the second hierarchy (kyriotetes, dynamis, and exusiai), within whom we live
for a certain period between death and rebirth. We develop a
special relationship with them by penetrating the Earth's memories along the path of light of its veins of metal. Here again,
however, we can understand our earthly experiences of the metals only when we have crossed over into the region of the second
hierarchy.

You see, one of the most beautiful experiences we can have is to
be able to investigate the various relationships between metals
and human health. And I have reason to hope that the anthroposophic movement will be particularly successful in uncovering the
beauty to be found in this area of research. Every metal and metal
compound has a specific connection to human health. As we go

through life and experience health and illness, we continually form ties to the metals and their compounds that give the Earth its memories.

We must go beyond merely theorizing about the healing properties of lead and copper and their compounds and so on. These substances all constitute significant and valuable remedies if we know how to prepare them correctly. We must not be satisfied with talking in abstractions about the wonderful relationships between metals and the human being. Indeed, a feeling of reverence arises in us even now as we contemplate metallic veins in the Earth's depths. But we must go another step and develop a deep understanding of the marvelous connection between metals and the human being—a connection first revealed to us once we have examined it from the perspective of the human being in relation to health and illness.

As I suggested, it is hoped that much can be communicated to human hearts and minds through the anthroposophic movement in connection with this knowledge, since it is extremely important. In the past it was not so important, because humankind had an inherent sense of all these relationships; they recognized that the lead process is related to this or that in the human head, and they knew the connections involved in the silver process. The ancients spoke often of such matters. People of more recent times may read about this but fail to understand a word of it, because it is approached from a modern scientific perspective as though it were merely vague and empty abstractions.

Anthroposophic knowledge can deepen the mind and soul through contemplating the wonderful relationship between the metals and human health and illness. Thus, when we die we can take with us into the spiritual world something to help us understand, in a very special way, the language of the second hierarchy. As a result of such preparation here on Earth, we will take with us the necessary understanding so that the most profound mysteries of the universe can be revealed to us. This is a fact; we learn what anthroposophy teaches us not merely out of curiosity, but for its results once we have passed through the gate of death. Spiritual science offers us exactly what we need to find the right relationship with the beings we encounter between death and rebirth. Because those beings make up the world that will then surround us, our whole being must find a connection with them.

Thus, it is possible to present a detailed image of how we find such a relationship with those beings of the higher hierarchies between death and a new birth. But there is something else related to this as we pass through those regions, for which we will be well-prepared by our understanding of what has just been described. Now we must describe another experience.

Nature will reveal her mysteries to us if we can understand the relationship between Earth's metals and human health and illness. But there is something else involved in those secrets of nature. First we hear the beings of the second hierarchy speak of the nature of one or another metallic element—gold, silver, lead, copper, and so on. On Earth, we have a certain relationship to the great spiritual world when we first learn to read. And it dawns on us that by reading we can begin to penetrate many mysteries of the world, which might otherwise remain beyond our knowledge. (Of course, I am using this metaphor for comparison only, because, as an earthly experience, there is really nothing special in this process.) Through the beings of the second hierarchy at a certain point in our passage through the life after death, we familiarize ourselves with the language describing the metals and their connection with human health and illness. This language becomes what it should only when we can raise it from the level of prose in the spiritual cosmos to that of cosmic poetry, or more accurately, when we are able to lift *ourselves* to cosmic poetry.

Initially, we are largely a tabula rasa in relation to poetry. On Earth we can come to understand the voice, the rhythm, and the whole artistic form of verse, unless we lack all feeling for poetry. Likewise, when we ascend from dry prose to the poetry of the world beyond the threshold, we rise from speech of the second hierarchy (telling us of the relationship between the metals and human health) to an understanding of the mysteries of cosmic moral existence. This moral life encompasses not only human souls, but also the divine souls of all the hierarchical beings. And the mysteries of the soul element are opened to us especially in this region.

Then we can take another step. We can experience what I described as going up into the mountains and into the Earth's depths. Everything remains still at first—we observe the quiet veins of metal and the stone along the mountain ridges. But we can go farther and try not to view things only from a dry, utilitarian perspective (though we should not underrate that kind of observation, since we need to plant both feet firmly on the ground if we want to enter the suprasensory world, healthy in body and spirit). We can try to not stop short at what is thus far revealed to us but, instead, continue by observing metals melting in a fiercely hot fire, and how they change from a solid to a liquid. By visiting a foundry, for example, we see iron in the furnaces as it is made to flow radiantly, or witness the processes in which metal ores such as antimony are transformed not only from solid to liquid, but gradually into other states. As the metals are subjected to fire, we can allow what happens to them to affect us, and thus something quite new and different impresses the spiritual insight we have nurtured, and we develop a tremendously profound impression of the mysteries of our own existence.

I have often referred to this by saying that we should consider human beings in comparison to animals. The various kinds of anatomical comparisons made today—human and animal bones, muscles, and even blood—do reveal certain affinities.

But human superiority to animals becomes evident only when we consider the fact that the spines of animals are, for the most part, parallel with the Earth's surface, whereas that of the human being is vertical. Or consider our marvelous possession of language, with which the animals are not gifted, and go on from there to our capacity to think, which is developed from speech. When we observe how speaking and thinking develop in children and how their whole orientation in life begins with attaining an upright posture, we witness the activity of the marvelous forces whereby children find their way dynamically into the world. We see how the orientation of a child's limbs expresses itself in the melody and articulation of speech. If we observe how we actually build and shape ourselves in the world of the senses, we see formative forces quietly at work. It is indeed wonderful to see a child's growth as months pass—seeing the progress from crawling to upright walking and the adjustment of the whole orientation of the child's body and limbs to the world's dynamics, and then the formation of speech and thinking from the physical being.

With the mind at rest, we can contemplate this in all its wonder, watching the quiet majesty with which it presents itself to the observer. We observe a child learning to walk and talk and think, and it seems to be the most beautiful thing one can witness in human life. We gather impressions of this beautiful element in human life, and then, on the other hand, we can also witness the melting of metals when exposed to fire. We perceive the spiritual archetype of this in children, which leads them to learn to walk and speak. The archetype of this power is revealed when flames take hold of the metal, making it flow. As the metal becomes more fluid, it becomes more volatile, and we have a clearer perception of the inner resemblance between that process—which is, in fact, metal's destiny—and the smelting and volatilizing process in cosmic fires that enable a little child to walk, speak, and think. And we realize that the beings of the first hierarchy (the seraphim, cherubim, and thrones) are involved in a twofold activity.

One aspect of this is that they speak to us from the spiritual world into which we pass midway through our life between death and a new birth, where they reveal the mysteries of planetary and other cosmic activities (as I have described during the last few days). They also work down into the visible world. Here, in the visible realm, the influences of the seraphim, cherubim, and thrones are active, on the one hand, in little children as they learn to walk, speak, and think and, on the other hand, in everything behind the Earth's process in which fire plays a role, such as when fire melts glowing metals.

Our planet Earth is indeed built up through the melting and glowing of metals in the forces of fire. As we look back to ancient times when this planet Earth was being built, we see in the metal melting through the forces of fire an aspect of the works of the seraphim, cherubim, and thrones in the earthly world—in particular, how the beings of the first hierarchy accomplish this work, supported primarily by the thrones. We can look back into the ancient times of Earth and see how metals glowed and liquefied as they were subjected to the forces of fire, and how they played a special role in the Earth's manifestation. The thrones had an especially active role in this, with the seraphim and cherubim quietly working alongside. It is the cherubim, however, who play the main role when children learn to walk, talk, and think. But it is always the beings of the first hierarchy that we see working harmoniously in both of these activities.

This kind of knowledge links earthly death with resurrection in our life beyond the threshold. Such knowledge reveals the kinship between the cosmic fires by which metals are melted and the powers that make us truly human; thus the whole world becomes one and we realize that our earthly life between birth and death is really no different than our life in the spiritual world beyond the threshold. Life between death and a new birth is a metamorphosis of earthly life. We know how one becomes the other, and thus how one is merely a different form of the other. When such insights lift our souls, more are added along with them.

Indeed, these other insights can also come in another way. Try to imagine what I have been describing today as the wonderful relationship between the way fire forces melt and vaporize metals and the process of children learning to walk and speak and think. If you meditate on this in such a way that it deepens you inwardly, a force will take hold of your soul that allows you to solve a great mystery of life, so that the soul is developed and enriched. I am speaking of the functioning of karma, or destiny, in the human being. We can come to a real understanding of human destiny and karma through the twofold experience of seeing a child learning to walk, talk, and think, on the one hand, and the melting and vaporizing of metals subjected to fire, on the other. Karma is revealed in the fiery smelting of metals and in the appropriate transformation of a child's animal nature into human nature while learning to walk, talk, and think. Karma is the suprasensory element that reaches into our immediate, active human life.

As we progress in our meditation, we come to understand the mysteries of destiny that weave through our life. On the one hand, we have a picture of the destiny of metals as they are subjected to fire, and on the other, the destiny of the primal human being descending to Earth and learning to walk, talk, and think. Between these images we find what we need to know of the mystery of karma for our human life.

So you see, the suprasensory human being speaks into the human world of the senses about the matter of human destiny. This is what I wanted to speak to you about as part of our study of the suprasensory human being. We could never base such a study on abstract theories. To understand the human being, we must reach into all the mysteries involved in the being of nature as well as in the spirit of the cosmos. Ultimately, human beings are intimately connected with *all* the mysteries of nature and universal spirit. The human being is in fact a universe in miniature. But we must not imagine that whatever happens on a grand scale out in the macrocosm occurs in the same way in the microcosm. As the metals melt, majestic flames of the fire's forces flow out to the very limits of macrocosmic space—and such boundaries *do* exist.

My dear friends, try to picture these fiery forces through which metals become fluid and volatile. This vaporized substance radiates into the vast expanses of the universe, but it returns in the forces of light and its warmth. And as it returns from cosmic space, it takes hold of a child who can only crawl and helps that child to stand upright and walk. So we see the upward flow of currents in melting metals; they turn around when they have gone far enough out into the cosmos and return as the forces that lift a child into uprightness. What we see on the one hand, we find also on the other. This gives you a picture of the ascending and descending cosmic forces of metamorphosis and transformation that work in the spirit of the cosmos.

Now you will also be able to understand the true meaning of something else related to the knowledge of ancient times—the old practice of sacrifice. People sent their sacrificial flame, along with what they burned within it, out into vast cosmic space to the gods, so that it might return to work in the human world. The attitude of the priestly sage toward the sacrificial fire may be expressed in these words: "O flame, I commit to you what is mine on Earth. As the smoke ascends, may the gods accept it. May what is borne upward by flame become divine blessing, poured again upon the Earth as creative, fructifying power."

As we hear the words of those ancient, sacrificial priests, who spoke of suprasensory worlds, we realize that they, too, were speaking of the cosmic mysteries of which we are a part.

My dear friends, this is what I wanted to say to you about our suprasensory nature as human beings, as it is understood by spiritual science.

Afterword

Paul Margulies

1. Image of the Human Being

"We are all slaves of our own self-image," wrote C. G. Jung with a sledgehammer. How we see ourselves affects every aspect of our lives. It colors our moods. It determines our attitudes toward life, our relationships, every turn of our behavior. How much strength did Steiner himself derive from his unshakable view of the human being as spirit enveloped in a spiritual world? And what are the consequences to the life of one who embraces materialism? Are we a chance collection of molecules as materialistic science would have us think? Do we see ourselves as a speck of dust on a speck of dust hurtling through the universe with "delirious rapidity?" Recent discoveries seem to support this view. Upsilon Andromedae, forty-four light years away, now appears as the center of another "solar system" with three planets in orbit, two of them with masses much greater than that of Jupiter. And astronomers are confident that this is the first of many similar discoveries.

Do we see ourselves as creatures of a purely natural world, devoid of moral impulses, a "higher animal" subject to the evolutionary law of "survival of the fittest?" Even "higher" has come into doubt. The natural-scientific community was willing to accept a distinction between humans and animals based on the fact that human beings could create "culture," an environment for learning that could be passed on from adult to child, with the possibility for *improvement*, for the progress of culture. But anthropologists now contend that there is a "culture" in the animal kingdom, for example, chimpanzees communicate information to immature chimpanzees through "teaching techniques" in which behavior is learned that is beyond inborn, instinctive behavior.

With the advent of genetic engineering there is even a materialistic view of "immortality." We know that embryonic stem cells are undifferentiated germ cells capable of limitless multiplication. Normally they specialize to become the cells of a particular organ. At that point they become subject to mortality. The goal of research in this field is to "trick" the stem cells into specializing while retaining their immortal genetic characteristics. If this goal is reached, we could stay young forever. We could cheat death. And then what?

What do we do with heartfelt ideals such as truth, goodness, beauty? Nobility, dignity, selflessness? Do we interpret these ideals as "survival mechanisms," strategies of enlightened self-interest, so that we can squeeze them into our Darwinian preconceptions? Do we try to live up to them, to soar with them into the vast regions of the spiritual worlds as companions to the gods? Do we lose ourselves in the warm air of our own wishes as seekers of bliss? Or do we sink into the cynicism or despair that awaits the pure materialist? "What is this materialism, really?" Steiner asks. "Materialism is a worldview that sees the human being as a product of physical substances and forces" (page 20). The issue is not to contradict materialism, but to recognize "the tremendous weight and power" of it, and to balance that power with a "true science of the soul and spirit based, just as ancient spiritual knowledge was, on *observation* and *experience* of the spirit" (page 22).

Keep in mind that Rudolf Steiner was never an enemy of natural science. His whole education was grounded in natural science, and included his graduation from the esteemed Technical School of

Vienna, which might be compared to M.I.T. today. "It is not my intention to say anything against [natural scientific] knowledge. It has achieved the very greatest success in its own territory, and, from an external point of view, has brought the human race extraordinary blessings" (PL II 2).[1] And he begins lecture 1 of this book: "We will go right to work by looking at the human being honestly, just as modern science does, and thus something will then reveal itself to us. Using all that physiology, biology, chemistry, and other sciences can contribute to our understanding of the human being, we will learn how the various substances and forces of the Earth come together to build muscles, nervous system, circulatory system, and the various senses.... What do we know about the human being? We must say that we know a great deal.... But when we turn to psychologists, whose vocation is to understand the soul, we encounter an atmosphere of doubt and uncertainty" (page 21).

This "atmosphere of doubt and uncertainty" still pervades the teachings of even the greatest psychologists, like C. G. Jung who points wisely to "archetypes" guiding the human soul. Still...these archetypes are felt as abstractions...the stuff of dreams...myths. And Viktor Frankl, whose "logotherapy," based on finding *meaning* in one's life, comes right up to the door of anthroposophy, but cannot enter.

> How does a human being go about *finding* meaning? As Charlotte Buhler has stated: "All we can do is study the lives of people who seem to have found their answers to the questions of what ultimately human life is about as against those who have not." In addition to such a biographical approach, however, we may as well embark on a biological approach.[2]

---

1. See the key to this and all following references with initials at the end of the afterword, p. 137.
2. Viktor Frankl, *Man's Search for Meaning*, Washington Square Press, New York, 1984, pp. 169ff.

"We may as well" . . . still, not quite sure. Then, after discussing conscience as "a prompter which, if need be indicates the direction in which we have to move in a given life situation" evaluating the situation "in the light of a hierarchy of values," Frankl concludes that these values cannot be adopted by us on a conscious level. "They have crystallized in the course of the evolution of our species; they are founded on our biological past and are rooted in our biological depth." He thinks this is what Konrad Lorenz might have had in mind when he developed the concept of the biological *a priori.* Lorenz agreed. "In any case, if a pre-reflective axiological self-understanding exists, we may assume that it is ultimately anchored in our biological heritage." And doesn't Frankl see that this completely contradicts his entire work? If I am acting under a biological imperative, this drains my life of all meaning. What does it mean to be fully human if not that we create our own worth? If I am driven to a conscientious act by some biological imperative, why should I care? Unless we adopt values on a *conscious* level, what possible meaning can my life have?

There is in Steiner's anthroposophy indications for a path of development of consciousness that would recover for us the sources of meaning, that can bring us to the *reality,* the *experience* of Jung's archetypes. This developed consciousness lifts itself from ordinary objective self-consciousness to three higher levels called, technically, *imagination, inspiration,* and *intuition.* And as soon as one is able to accept this development of consciousness as a possibility, one can read with an open attitude what an initiate, such as Steiner, has to describe as experiences and observations of higher worlds.

For anthroposophy, the human being is composed of body, soul, and spirit. The distinction between soul and spirit is one of the main contributions of anthroposophy to an understanding of the human being. Steiner points to the year A.D. 869 when the spirit, formally acknowledged and taught in the Christian world, was eliminated from the image of the human being. It was then that the Ecumenical Council of Constantinople decreed that the human being was essentially body and soul, the soul having some attributes of the spirit, thus banishing the spirit from the image of the human being. Today the tendency is to deny the existence of the soul altogether, limiting the human being to "body." With this view our entire life of consciousness and feeling is seen as epiphenomena of the body, electrical nerve impulses responding to stimuli in the environment.

Anthroposophy understands body, soul, and spirit as interdependent during life on Earth, and also interpenetrating, so it is difficult to define them neatly. It helps to see the body as providing the sense organs for the *consciousness* of the soul, and the limbs to carry out the *intentions* of the spirit. The soul mediates between body and spirit, bringing information about the physical world to the spirit through its experiences. The soul is the locus of our feeling life, essentially sympathy and antipathy. Think of *longing* and you come close to pure soul. Follow this longing thoughtfully and you will experience it poised between body and spirit. Through instinct and sense perception, the soul works through the body. Through thinking, the soul expresses the spirit. The soul is individual, particular, personal. The spirit is universal, ideal, eternal. The spirit is expressed primarily in thinking, especially the kind of thinking that is capable of giving direction to the soul and the body toward that which it recognizes as ideal: truth, goodness, and beauty, for example, if we can get past these as cliches or mere abstractions. Real thinking, pure thinking, the spirit, has a transformative effect. Insofar as the soul is immersed in sense perception and unexamined impulses, it lives in the transient world. It is concerned only with itself. When the soul turns to thinking and ideals, it touches the eternal. Real thinking is universal. The will in our thinking is our own.[3] It is true that when the soul is concerned with the mundane and utilitarian, the thoughts about these things seem cold and abstract compared to the rich life of feelings. But the opposite is true of thoughts that lead to higher levels of existence.

> No feeling and no enthusiasm on Earth can compare with the sensations of warmth, beauty and exaltation that are enkindled by pure, crystal-clear thoughts relating to higher worlds. Our loftiest feelings are not the ones that happen by themselves, but the ones achieved through strenuous and energetic thinking....
>
> Through thinking, we are led beyond our own personal lives; we acquire something that extends beyond our own souls. We take it as a matter of course that the laws of thinking correspond with the universal order. We can feel at home in the universe because this correspondence exists, and it is a weighty factor in learning to recognize our own essential nature. We seek the truth in our soul; through this truth, not only the soul but also the things of the world express themselves. Truth recognized through thinking has an independent significance, which refers to the things of the world and not merely to our own souls (*Theosophy*, pp. 32, 43).[4]

Real thinking is imbued with both will and feeling. Real thinking is the starting point for anthroposophy ("a path of cognition"), and this distinguishes it from most other paths to the spirit.

In his book *Theosophy* (pp. 26–63), Steiner approaches the image of the human being from many points of view. After the basic image of the human being as body, soul, and spirit, one can look at a fourfold image of the human being composed of physical body, ehteric body, astral body, and I-being or ego.

Thus:

---

3. Rudolf Steiner, *The Bridge Between Universal Spirituality and the Physical Constitution of Man*, Anthroposophic Press, Hudson, NY, 1979, p. 49.
4. Steiner, *Theosophy*, Anthroposophic Press, Hudson, NY, 1994.

1. *Physical/mineral body,* which we have in common with the mineral kingdom;

2. *Etheric body, or body of formative forces,* which we have in common with the plant kingdom. This is the "body" that contains the forces that maintain our shape, just as the shape of a geranium leaf is always maintained in its uniqueness. The etheric body contains the life-forces characterized by nutrition, growth, and reproduction;

3. *Astral body, or soul body,* which we have in common with the animal kingdom. The astral body is the locus of our consciousness and our feelings;

4. *I-being,* or pure ego. This is unique to human beings, and separates us from the animal kingdom. Through the I, capable of thinking, we achieve self-awareness. This offers us the opportunity for self-transformation. We can develop in ourselves the capacity to transform the lower members of our being so that they evolve into their spiritual counterparts; thus:

5. *Spirit-self,* as the transformed astral body;

6. *Life-spirit,* as the transformed etheric body;

7. *Spirit-body,* as the transformed physical body.

We can also view the threefold human being of body, soul, and spirit as a ninefold human being with three bodily members (physical body, intellectual body, and astral body); three soul members (sentient soul, intellectual soul, and consciousness soul); and three spirit members (spirit self, life spirit, and spirit body).

Three bodily members (physical body, etheric body, and astral body);

Three soul members (sentient soul, intellectual soul, and consciousness soul);

Three spirit members (spirit self, life spirit, and spirit body).

Another idea central to the anthroposophic image of the human being is that of *reincarnation and karma*. Karma can be described as self-created destiny. The thoughts, feelings, and deeds of one life—our relationships to other people, events, and surroundings in this life—determine the talents, dispositions, places, and whom and what we meet in the next. Reincarnation refers to the eternal aspect of our innermost being, our true I, or higher self, the entity that reincarnates on Earth continuously for the purpose of evolving appropriately along with the evolving universe.

This is our continuous journey as a human spirit in the universe. We could say that the physical body is subject to the law of heredity, the soul is subject to the law of karma, and the spirit to the law of reincarnation.

We have already touched on the third aspect of the anthroposophic image of the human being, the capacity for self-transformation. The human being is never a *finished* object; he or she is always in the process of *becoming*. Every human being possesses slumbering organs of perception that can be awakened. These awakened soul-spiritual organs provide perception and experience of higher worlds. These higher states of consciousness (*imagination, inspiration,* and *intuition,* mentioned above) are attained through exercises in meditation and in practical life. The exercises lead to an intensification of our three basic faculties, thinking, feeling, and willing. "Study" is the first step. Even in grappling with this content right now, you are immersing yourself in spiritual ideas, and planting the seed of your spiritual being in a medium through which it can grow and develop. "Anthroposophical ideas are vessels fashioned by love, and our being is spiritually summoned by the spiritual world to partake of their content."[5]

We read in the first lecture that the human form can be seen through *imaginative* cognition in the planetary system. The human

---

5. Steiner, *Awakening to Community*, Anthroposophic Press, Hudson, NY, 1974, p. 6.

form is then contrasted to the animal form, which is not found in the planetary *system*, but in the *movements* of the planets. The crucial distinction is that the human being stands upright, aligned vertically with the cosmos, whereas the animal is always aligned horizontally to the Earth's surface. The animal copies the movements of the planets, which especially influence its skeleton and the form of the limbs. With *imaginative* cognition, one can even see the specific point in the spine where the Sun is active, where the spine shows a tendency to change into the head structure, "the point where the spine tends to transform into the head structure, which displays a transformed spinal vertebra. Saturn and Jupiter work at the point where the bones of the spine rise and 'puff out' ... to become skull bones" (page 35).

This spiritual image of the human being as described in these lectures—the skin, nervous system, cardiovascular system, musculature, and skeleton—is a picture of *forces*. At conception and birth these forces combine with earthly substances and forces.

> As human beings, we come down to Earth formed and fashioned by the heavens. Initially, we are wholly suprasensory, right to our very bones.... At death, we let it fall away again and retain our spirit form as we pass through the gate of death. (page 36).

2. Death as Transformation: Our Journey through the Universe

> Even if death means destruction when seen from the physical standpoint of life, it is the most glorious, lofty and beautiful thing of all when seen from the other side of life... There it constantly bears witness to the victory of the spirit over matter, to the self-creative vital power of the spirit. (LBD, pp. 104, 125)

After death, when freed from the physical body, we begin to experience the reality of our true self, the higher self, the pure *ego*, or I-being. During earthly life we needed to come up against the physical body in order to experience I-consciousness. We needed sensory impressions of the outer world to make us aware of ourselves. But in the spiritual world our own inner activity is so intense that we become aware of ourselves, and this awareness is anchored in our experience of death, of having left our physical body. We remember our death. We know we are an I because we know that we have shed our transient, physical member. We can now experience the reality of our spiritual being through its own vitality, unhindered by the physical body.

After death we see our true form, radiant and shining with the forces flowing from the archetype of the human being inscribed as the image in the planetary system. This radiant light body is illumined by our morality, serving as a constant judge, as a "physiognomy" which can be read like an open book. After death, no pretense is possible. We cannot hide our insincerity behind a phony smile or an evasive phrase. A bad person will not appear the same as a good person. "One who has made strenuous efforts during earthly life will not appear the same as one whose life was thoughtless or superficial" (page 40). This luminous image of our own form illuminating our earthly deeds exists within us during earthly life. This is what we experience as conscience.

Our first experience after death is that of seeing our entire life spread out before us as living pictures in a vast tapestry or memory tableau. Everything we experienced on Earth is there before us. This tableau lasts about three and a half days, during which our etheric body dissolves into the cosmic ether. We feel the pictures expanding as they are received by the universe, a spiritual counterpart of our lives, of everything we did or felt or thought on Earth. This spiritual counterpart of our lives is engraved into the world as part of the Akashic Record. (Those with initiate-consciousness can "read" this Akashic Record, the source of all of our great religious documents, the Old and New Testaments, the Vedas, the great world myths, and so on.) "There is no single experience whose spiritual counterpart is not engraved into the spiritual world in which we are ever present, even while on Earth. Every handshake we have exchanged has its spiritual counterpart; it is there, inscribed into the spiritual world" (LBD, p. 40).

Our journey through the planetary spheres follows the esoteric designations of the planets, expanding outward from the Earth, to the orbit of the Moon, then onward to Mercury, Venus, Sun, Jupiter, Saturn, passing finally through the fixed stars. (The positions of Mercury and Venus are transposed, again, following spiritual sight and esoteric tradition.[6]) The "sphere" of each planet is determined by its orbit as the outer limit, and the immediately preceding planet. The Moon sphere, then, is the space between the Earth and the orbit of the Moon (this book, p. 12 and LBD&NB, pp. 41ff).

After the memory tableau, we spend the first period of our life between death and a new birth in the Moon sphere. This is described in *Theosophy* as the soul world, composed essentially of desire, longing, and wishes. The two basic forces are sympathy and antipathy. Antipathy here is equivalent to self-centeredness, which is worth pondering. Our journey through the soul world is an ascension through distinct regions, separated according to the predominance of sympathy or antipathy. In the lowest level, antipathy prevails, and we ascend through regions of gradually diminishing antipathy, until there is no element of antipathy to overcome, until we are free of egotism (*Theosophy*, pp. 100–122).

The passage of the soul through the soul world is called the period of *purification, kamaloca* in Eastern esotericism, and *purgatory* in the theology of the West.[7] We move through the soul world by experiencing our life in reverse, from the moment we died, back to the moment of our birth, like a film run in reverse.

---

6. See Steiner, *The Spiritual Hierarchies and the Physical World*, Anthroposophic Press, Hudson, NY, 1996, lecture 6 and the essay by Georg Unger in the appendix.
7. This is the "period of trial" mentioned on p. 41.

And our experiences are also reversed. We experience not what we did to another, but what the other experienced as the result of our deed. For example, as we review our lives, coming to the experience of having slapped someone, instead of experiencing the satisfaction of "letting him have it," we feel the pain he or she felt. We experience a mirror of our own being. We impress on our souls especially the harm we have done to people, and the consequences of the passions in which we have indulged.

In *An Outline of Esoteric Science* Steiner describes three types of desire. The first type refers to appropriate desires that find their satisfaction in the physical world, the desire for food, for instance, which nourishes us and enables us to work in the world. The second type of desire is desire for the spirit, for example, desire for the truth, or to serve the community. The third type of desire is for things that can only find satisfaction in the physical world, through the physical body, but are completely devoid of spirit. This might have started out as a justifiable desire, but escalates to the point of immoderation, or excess. The gourmet, for instance, who spends a good part of his or her life in an extraordinary effort to please his or her taste buds. This pleasure is the focus of the desire, with little or no thought to the healthy nourishment for fruitful work in the world (OES, pp. 79ff).

We encounter these desires (empty of spirit) in the lowest region of the soul world, the *Region of Burning Desires*. This is the "land mass" of the soul world, characterized by insatiable greed and self-centeredness, with antipathy predominating. We carry our passions into this region, but if they can only be satisfied through the physical body, because we have no physical organs, for example, taste buds, they can find no satisfaction. The desire itself, far more intense than our desires on Earth, is experienced as a "burning thirst." And this "burning" continues until we give up the desire, until it is "burned" away. As we ascend in the soul world our various desires are "purified" in the appropriate regions. The second region, called the *Region of Flowing Sensitivity* (the seas and rivers of the soul world), finds antipathy and sympathy in balance. But this balance is characterized by a certain neutrality of the soul, which translates on Earth as not caring, or easily-swayed, or superficiality. The third region (air) is the *Region of Wishes*. Here sympathy predominates, but still, a certain amount of antipathy gives it a fundamental note of self-seeking. (I wish I were a movie star. I wish I could help you, but...) How much of our soul life on Earth do we bring to this region? In the fourth region (warmth), the *Region of Pleasure/Displeasure*, sympathy predominates to a greater extent. We are living in the realm of "feelings." Much of modern psychology is focused on this region. "Displeasure" here is seen as a lessening of "pleasure," defining our level of comfort.

It is not until we reach the fifth level of the soul world, the *Region of Pure Soul Light*, that we are able to overcome antipathy, egotism, and stand in complete sympathy for the "other." The "other" is received as information, as revelation. The active force is "light," illuminating the being and essence of the "other" for his or her own sake. Steiner names but does not describe the sixth and seventh regions of the soul world, *Soul Power*, and *Soul Life*. Starting with the fifth region (Soul Light), the soul experiences an enlightening, enlivening, and awakening of what would, if left to itself, become lost in its own existence.

Essentially, in the soul world we experience pain for the harmful deeds we have done and burning thirst for the inappropriate passions we have harbored. This continues until we have realized their worthlessness. And we are aware of suprasensory beings sharing our experience, "showering down their sympathies and antipathies upon our deeds and thoughts" like a spiritual rain (LBD, p. 40). We feel held in the gaze of these beings as if it would annihilate our very being. Though these experiences are painful, we accept them with gratitude, even bliss, depending on our maturity. We know that through this painful compensation we are developing as human beings, that without it we would fall short of our full humanity.

These experiences gradually lead to a force, an impulse proceeding from the spiritual beings surrounding us, a realization that we have acted either according to their intentions or against them. We realize that we have either contributed to the evolution of the world, or hindered it. This evaluation is the reality of our existence when we enter the spiritual world after death. We feel the gaze of these spiritual beings upon us, we feel their sympathy, we realize we have attained our full reality as soul-spiritual beings. And we realize that *our reality depends upon our value.* If we feel that we have hindered evolution, we feel a darkness robbing us of our very being. If we have done something to foster evolution, "it is as if light were calling us to a fresh spiritual life" (LBD, p. 48).

The spirit is set free as soon as the soul surrenders to dissolution everything it can experience only in the body, retaining those experiences that led the soul on Earth to consider the world of spirit. This "remainder" is imprinted on the spirit as "the fruits of a lifetime," and links the soul to the spirit in the spirit world (*Theosophy*, p. 112). After purification and our entry into the spirit world, our only desires are for the spirit. Life's fruits, this spiritual yield that becomes an essential part of us, is the very purpose of our having been born on Earth.

Our capacity for consciousness throughout our journey through the planetary spheres corresponds, to begin with, to the inner forces we bring with us. Our awareness is due to an inner light gleaned from the fruits of our struggles on Earth, the gratitude with which we accepted the joy that came to us, our inner strength of soul. This becomes the luminous, radiating spiritual "physiognomy" as mentioned. Through this inner light the outer spiritual world becomes visible to us. We become aware that had we not developed this inner light everything in the spiritual world would remain dark. As we encounter the beings and processes of the spiritual world a power of soul awakens, a creativity of will permeated by intense feeling. We feel ourselves to be a creative part of the universe through which the spiritual world is streaming. "The lights for the life beyond must be carried upward from the Earth" (LBD, p. 202).

Thus, the shortcomings we bring with us from the Earth dim our consciousness in the various planetary spheres, while our spiritual development during our earthly life illuminates our spiritual surroundings. Our urges, passions, emotions, and sensual love absorb us in the Moon sphere. In Mercury we meet our moral imperfections. In the Venus sphere we meet our religious shortcomings. In the Sun sphere, the sphere of the universal human being, we become aware of everything that prevented us from becoming fully human. We meet our self-centeredness, our identifying with an ethnic group, a nation, or a religion to the exclusion of others.

After our sojourn in the soul world (the Moon sphere), we enter the first region of the spirit world, the Mercury sphere. Here we come together with family and friends. But if we lacked a moral sense in life, a barrier is created that prevents us from reaching them. A soul with an immoral disposition becomes a hermit here, an isolated being. Death does not exist in the spiritual world, only transformation. The equivalent of death in the spiritual world is loneliness, a loneliness that is far more intense than any experienced on Earth. As a general rule (there are many exceptions) we incarnate twice during a 2,160 year period. This is the time it takes for the sun to pass through a constellation, as measured by the vernal equinox. In that time conditions on Earth have changed radically enough for us to garner completely new experiences. During that time we incarnate once as a male, once as a female, again, to gather the different experiences provided by the difference in gender. Therefore, we spend about 1,000 years in the spiritual world between incarnations (OES, pp. 404ff). Should we fail on Earth to develop the capacities that would make us sociable beings in the spiritual world, this would entail centuries of loneliness. Thus, to be sociable beings in the Mercury sphere, we had to be moral on Earth (LBD&NB, pp. 283ff). In the Mercury sphere, our love for family and friends is deepened, and our capacities in this direction enhanced.

During earthly life, if we have caused someone harm, we have many opportunities to correct that mistake. But in the spiritual world that is no longer possible. We remain cut off from the person we have injured. And if we didn't love someone enough on Earth, we have no opportunity to compensate for this in the spiritual world. We can bring only as much affection to the other as we held during physical life. We experience this incapacity to compensate for failures during earthly life as an immense weight on our souls. We feel as if chained to the ground (LBD&NB, pp. 64ff, 83ff, 108, 130). We realize that in order to avoid mistakes in the future, we must return to the physical plane to develop our inner powers further. Thus an impulse for improvement in this direction is implanted in our souls.

We don't merely enhance our capacities for relationships in the spiritual world, but we live into the wisdom of the cosmos. In *Theosophy*, Steiner describes the planetary spheres as the dwelling places of the archetypes. In the Mercury sphere we meet the archetypes for everything manifesting as physical on Earth; these are the "land masses" of the spiritual world. We find ourselves surrounded by thoughts, but these thoughts, the archetypes, are real *beings*. One of the thoughts we meet here is the idea of our own physical body. In earthly life we identify with our body, but here we realize that our body does not belong to us; it belongs to the outer world. We experience the outer world as a unity, and our physical body as part of that unity, merging with the unity of the world. Gradually we become aware of our relationship to that unity; we realize that we ourselves once were what is here spread out before us. This is what is meant in the Vedanta idea: "Thou art that." This is an ideal in earthly life, but in this region of the spiritual world we *experience* it as a reality. We feel ourselves as spirits among spirits, as organs of primal spirits. We experience in ourselves their word: "I am the primal spirit (I am Brahman)." I am part of, an organ of, the primal spirit from whom all beings spring (*Theosophy*, p. 135). The idea can be thought on Earth because it is an actual fact in the spiritual world.

In the Venus sphere we expand the circle of our community to include those with whom we have shared a common religious life. If we lacked any religious inclination on Earth we become hermits. A materialist lives here in painful isolation. The groupings tend to follow those on Earth because so many religious creeds are associated with nations. Religious confessions and philosophies held in common form powerful communities in the Venus sphere. Here we enhance our capacities for devotion to the whole, toward the unity and harmony of the world. This devotion is the basis of religious life. We see the personal and transitory as an *image* of something *eternal*, of a harmonious whole, and "we look up to this unity reverently and worshipfully in our religious rituals.... Religious feeling and everything in us that struggled for a pure and noble morality draws strength from this region." This second region of the spiritual world is the dwelling place of the archetypes of life. These archetypes flow as a fluid element, the *rivers and seas* of the spiritual world. On Earth, life appears bound to individual living things, but in the spiritual world life is released from individual entities and flows as the blood of life, as a living unity present in all things (*Theosophy*, pp. 138ff).

In the Sun sphere our community expands to include all of humanity. Anything that prevented us from recognizing our universal humanness hinders our consciousness here. From this region we draw forces that build up our etheric bodies in the next incarnation. These forces flow from the element common to all religions. Each religion was appropriate for a given place and time, for a different stage of consciousness developing in a particular cultural epoch. True Christianity speaks to the universal human being. It is the goal of the *Mystery of Golgotha* (Steiner's term for the passion, death, and resurrection of Jesus Christ), through spiritual science, to unite all religions in peace all over the world. We have not yet reached the stage of realizing that a Buddhist or a Hindu, a Moslem or a Jew, can recognize the Christ. We must come to the understanding that Christ died for the whole of humanity, that Christ lives in every single human being (LBD&NB pp. 67ff, 91ff, 136ff, 275ff, 288). This is not a creed, but a fact perceptible to initiate consciousness. By the same token, adherence to any of the major religions cannot either defeat nor guarantee the ability to reach this understanding. In the Sun sphere, the "atmosphere" of the spirit world, we meet the archetypes of soul. *Feeling* exists in the spirit world as an all-pervading presence like air on Earth. We are asked to imagine a sea of flowing feeling, of sorrow and pain, joy and delight, flowing through this realm like winds and storms. If we imagine a battle on Earth and eliminate everything physical, holding our gaze on the feelings alone—the passions confronting passions, the pain, the joy of conquest—these are seen as a raging thunderstorm.

At this point in our journey, no egotism clings to the soul. We live in this flowing feeling common to all human souls, just as all human beings breathe the same air. What I desire is indistinguishable from what my fellow human being desires. My wish is your wish. We are universal human beings. Everything that serves the common good, our selfless devotion to others, bears fruit in this region. The great benefactors of mankind acquire their gifts here, having prepared themselves in previous lifetimes (*Theosophy*, p. 140).

In the Mars sphere, the fourth region of the spirit world, we enter a realm of thoughts penetrating everything in the spirit world like "warmth" pervading the Earth. Here we meet the *governing* archetypes, the "archetypes of archetypes." In the three lower regions of the spirit world we met with the archetypes of the "given," of the things in the world we find in existence before our intervention as human beings. Here we meet with the archetypes of the "possible," the archetypes, therefore, of purely human creations. Our life on Earth is related to the "given," to the transient things that point us to their place in the eternal. But we bring something new to the world. Think of all the human creativity expressed in the arts and sciences, in agriculture and technology, in government and law. These are original works of the human spirit.

Artists, scientists, scholars, and inventors enhance their capacities in the Mars sphere. Here we each develop our impulses to transcend the transient, to reach beyond the narrow confines of our personal lives, to touch universal human concerns (*Theosophy*, p. 140).

In the spiritual world, our awareness has been both a "seeing" and a "hearing." Other senses come into play as well, but Steiner's descriptions involve only this "seeing" and "hearing" (*Theosophy* p. 126). In the Sun sphere, for instance, we were immersed in "the harmony of spheres," a harmony, melody, and rhythm expressing the cooperation of all the beings of the hierarchies. Everything is sounding out of the cosmos, but always in harmonies, as opposed to the separate sounds we hear on Earth. In the Mars sphere, cosmic music becomes cosmic speech. We participate in the mystery of the Word, the creative word from which all things become manifest (LBD&NB, p. 21).

Another aspect of our passage through Mars concerns the Buddha, whose mission was to redeem Mars in a way analogous to the Christ's redemption of Earth. Steiner points to a "crucifixion" of Buddha on Mars early in the seventeenth century A.D. Mars had always been connected with aggressive, warlike elements, with rivalries of souls perpetually clashing. These impulses were imparted to human souls on their return to the Earth, to be expressed in the coming incarnation. Since Buddha's "crucifixion" on Mars, he has been able to temper this aggressiveness with peace and harmony. Now human souls are able to absorb Buddhistic impulses on Mars for their next incarnation (LBD&NB, pp. 204ff, 248ff).

In the fifth, sixth, and seventh regions (Jupiter, Saturn, the fixed stars) we move into the realm of *intentions* and *goals*. We ascend into a purely spiritual world where we can actually experience the aims we have set for our earthly lives, in accordance with the intentions of the hierarchies. Everything on Earth is a mere copy of the intentions and goals established in these regions. Every crystal, plant, animal, and human achievement is a pale copy of an intention that rose in the spirit world (*Theosophy*, p. 142).

In the Jupiter sphere (the fifth region) we experience our true self, the spirit-self, the entity that assumes earthly existence incarnation after incarnation. We live in this realm of intentions like an architect learning from past mistakes, discarding the results of experiences that have to do with transient imperfections. The strength we draw from this region depends on how far we have developed on Earth, how much our worldly experiences have borne fruit for the spirit. How have we passed our earthly tests? The richest yields always come from the way we resolve the difficulties that come to meet us. The deeper the crisis, the greater the opportunity for spiritual yield. Two of the qualities developed on Earth that bear fruit here are an active thought life and wise, loving work. Lacking these qualities, we feel an urgent need to make up this deficit in the next life, so that the effect of this deficit becomes clear in the karma we meet. Our greatest struggles, the "bitter fate" that brings us so much pain, is seen from the Jupiter sphere as exactly what we need. As the true self develops it will seek its home in this region more and more. In future incarnations it will live more and more in harmony with the spiritual intentions and goals developed here (*Theosophy,* pp. 143ff).

In *An Outline of Esoteric Science,* Steiner refers to Jupiter as the "Realm of Spiritual Light." Wisdom reveals itself in its primal form, wisdom, shining like the Sun, revealing true meaning, the "true colors" of every object it shines upon (OES, p. 94). Now the cosmos begins to work powerfully on us through the "Harmony of the Spheres." This increases in volume until we are dazed by it (LBD&NB, p. 22). We are in the company of mighty thought-beings, who are radiating thoughts into the planetary system. Together with them, and with other human souls, we work on fashioning the spiritual seed for what will become our head in our next incarnation. The head is fashioned first so we can understand the cosmos through the cosmic thoughts that begin to live in the head (page 79).

Ascending to Saturn, we increase our understanding of spiritual goals and intentions. We realize why we act for what is best for the evolution of the world, and not for our own good. We are now in the sphere of "cosmic memory" amongst mighty spiritual beings who preserve the memory of everything that happens on Earth. We realize how little our life on Earth was attuned to the higher moral demands of the spirit, how far we departed from knowing the real majesty and harmony of the universe. Our past life is seen as a reproach. We become painfully aware of our failure to live up to our intended goals. (LBD&NB, p. 22)

This region is especially significant for those who studied spiritual science. The forces acquired through immersing oneself in spiritual thoughts are transformed in the Saturn sphere into forces that elaborate a bodily constitution that will provide a natural inclination toward the spirit in the next earthly life. Such a person will be receptive to spiritual science no matter what the earthly environment. Once established, there is progress through incarnations until this spiritual inclination becomes clear even in childhood. It is a spiritual law that what has been absorbed as conceptual life in one lifetime appears as *impulse* or *force* in the next. John the Baptist, for example, completely immersed in spiritual thought, reappears as Raphael in a subsequent incarnation, with forces that enabled him to paint the deeply provocative and beautiful figures of Christianity (LBD&NB, pp. 255ff).

In the Mars sphere we learned the speech of gods; in the Jupiter sphere we learned the thought of gods; in the Saturn sphere we learn the memory of gods.

Ascending now into the seventh region, the fixed stars, we enter the totality of cosmic forces that elaborate the spirit germ of our next incarnation. As we approach this midpoint of our journey, our outer perception grows fainter, while, at the same time, our inner experience grows richer. At midpoint, we fall into a spiritual sleep. At this "midnight hour" we experience a most intense feeling of being within ourselves, an awareness of *knowing* that is almost unbearable because it is only knowing, and—because it is only knowing—we know that we are shut off from the outer world. It is as if we are told: "You carry a world within you which you experience only by knowing, a world from whose reality you are shut off; you have lost the power of illuminating it" (LBD, p. 27). The spiritual beings and powers were first sensed through spiritual vision, then heard as the harmony of spheres created through a cosmic orchestra, then as a cosmic chorus, and then as the cosmic word. Now we "fall asleep" and the spiritual forces of the entire universe penetrate us. The work on the spiritual head is completed. Impulses pour in from spiritual realms.

Our unbearable sense of isolation develops into a longing for the outer world. This longing becomes a new power, an active force that creates for itself an outer world. Images of our previous incarnations arise. Our past surrounds us. We judge it. Our outward journey was an expansion into the universe up to the "midnight hour." Our return is a contraction. During our outward journey, our perfections and imperfections were inscribed into the appropriate planetary spheres (LBD&NB, p. 253). The longing arises to compensate for our deficiencies. We realize that this can occur only in a new life on Earth. This creates an instinctive urge for a new birth. We encounter the *thirst for existence*. And we begin our return. On our return we will meet what we ourselves inscribed in the various regions, and these will be incorporated into our developing body and soul constitutions. Those souls will reappear with whom we are linked by destiny. We will judge what we still owe them, we will plan what we can create together. We will envision the souls with whom we shared religious or philosophical inclinations. We will impress upon ourselves ideal figures we wish to emulate, we will implant personal ideals. These experiences will provide the strength for our return (LBD & NB, p. 27).

When we return to Saturn, the foundation is laid for the faculty of memory we will need on Earth; cosmic memory is transformed into human memory. The spiritual seed for the head is developed further. This is a wonderful activity, one human being working on another in harmony with the beings of the hierarchies. This work reflects the creation of the world:

> Every individual human head is seen as a wonderful world, one of infinite variety and detail. And this work requires the devotion of human beings linked by destiny, along with the cooperation and necessary effort of hierarchical beings who understand, out of the mysteries of the cosmos, how to form the human head (page 80).

The work of the spiritual template for our bodily constitution continues on our return to Jupiter. Here the thoughts of gods are transformed into the faculty for human thinking. Returning through the Mars sphere we develop the spiritual seeds of a new body, particularly the structures of the limbs and chest, the larynx and the lung.

We then return to the Sun sphere. On our journey outward our whole being was surrendered to the cosmos. We learned cosmic speech, cosmic thoughts, cosmic memory. We united with the cosmos. Now, in the Sun sphere, we begin to separate out as individuals. The foundation is laid for the heart. Hints of a physical heart are "interwoven with our entire worth as individual human beings as a result of prior earthly lives ... this heart seed concentrates our whole moral being—our qualities of soul and spirit" (page 82). This leads to a sublime experience, difficult to put in words. Just as we feel intimately connected with our physical heartbeat,

> through our microcosmic spiritual heart we feel united with our whole being of soul and spirit. The moral being of soul and spirit that we have become at this moment of experience is a "spiritual heartbeat" within us. Our whole being thus seems to be in the cosmos, just as our heartbeat is in us (page 83).

This work of fashioning the human body from cosmic forces is the most awe-inspiring process imaginable. Through working together with other human souls spiritual relationships are formed that lead human beings to find each other in the coming incarnation. And its meaning is far greater than that of any human work done on Earth. After death, as a spirit among spirits, the world spread out around us is actually our organism, just as on Earth we find ourselves surrounded by mountains, trees, meadows, lakes and clouds, rivers and stars. Anatomists describe the organs and processes of the human body in great detail. And these are marvelous.

> But what lies within the human skin are great worlds ... in every human organ *whole universes are compressed into miniature forms....* If you survey what lies in a single pulmonary vesicle, it will appear more grandiose than the whole range of the mighty Alps. For what lies inside the human being is the whole spiritual cosmos in condensed form....

As here we found rocks, rivers, mountains on all sides, so there above we find the human being, humanity, on all sides. *Humankind is the world....* Just as on Earth we build machines, keep books, sew clothes, make shoes, write books, thus weaving together what is called the content of civilization, of culture, so above, together with the spirits of the higher hierarchies and incorporeal human beings, we weave the warp and weft of humankind. (LBD & NB, pp. 56–58).

We rightly praise the work of human beings in creating an earthly culture.

But a much more encompassing, a much more exalted, a much more magnificent work than all earthly cultural activity is performed by heavenly civilization ... between death and a new birth: the spiritual preparation, the spiritual weaving of the human body.... Not without justification did the ancient mysteries call the human physical body a *temple* (ibid., pp. 59–60).

Passing through Venus and Mercury we develop the spiritual seeds of our other organs. And here we arrange our destiny in terms of the family and nation into which we will be born so as to provide us with the appropriate opportunities for fulfilling our karma.

Finally, we return to the Moon sphere. The period of time spent here is equivalent to the time between earthly conception and birth, and here we retrieve the soul qualities, healthy and unhealthy, we inscribed here during the period of purification of the passions, urges, desires and sensuality we still have to struggle with. Thus the human embryo is developing along parallel lines with our cosmic development. We then see a preview of our coming life, more in terms of opportunities than as a finished product. At this point, our spiritual consciousness is again dimmed, and this dimmed consciousness is transformed into "the forces of growth in a dreamy, little child." The being of soul and spirit unites with the physical substances and forces provided by the embryo (page 86). A human being, in the flesh, begins a new life on Earth.

3. Affirmation of Life: Personal Responsibility

Anthroposophy never undervalues sensory existence. To the contrary, it insists that only in the sense world can we carry out our development in line with the goals of the spirit.

> The more we learn to rejoice in the physical world, the more deeply we enter into all the joy that the sense world bestows and the greater the measure of understanding that we bring to the realm of the angels. They are waiting to tell us of the mysteries here on Earth that we cannot yet understand, but that we do understand once we pass into the supraphysical realm (page 97).

This interlocking of the physical and the spiritual has always been a part of spiritual science.

> When you recall what the initiates and masters of various ages offered for the perfection and dignity of human life, you find that they never diminished the beauty, splendor, and majesty of our earthly life of the senses.... We have only to recall such images as the lotus flower to see that initiates never shied from depicting the spiritual development through images grounded in sensory experience, and that it was their belief that what we find—or at least *can* find—in the world of the senses leads to the highest (page 89).

And in *An Outline of Esoteric Science* Steiner writes:

> Even as a spirit being, the I *must* have sensory pleasures as long as it lives in a body. The spirit manifests in sense-perceptible things,

and the I is enjoying nothing other than the spirit when it gives itself up to sense-perceptible things through which the light of the spirit shines. The I will come to enjoy this light even when sense perception is no longer the medium for the rays of the spirit (OES, p. 81).

This clarifies the meaning of our life on Earth. It is only through our earthly sensory experiences that we develop—through our own effort—an understanding of the spiritual world, which is not "out there" somewhere, but right here, in our earthly experiences. An attentive sensory life brings us closer to the spirit, and an understanding of the spirit infinitely enhances our sensory existence.

Whenever I observe a stone, plant, animal or person, I should be aware that something eternal is expressed there. I should be able to wonder about what is lasting in a transitory stone or a mortal person, what it is that will outlast their transient sense-perceptible manifestation.

We must not imagine that if we turn our mind to the eternal like this, it will estrange us from immediate reality and destroy our ordinary capacity for observation and our feeling for everyday affairs. On the contrary! Each little leaf and beetle will reveal countless mysteries when we look at it not only with our eyes but also, through our eyes, with our spirit as well. Every glimmer or shade of color, every intonation, will remain vividly perceptible to our senses. Nothing will be lost, but infinite new life will be gained (*Theosophy*, pp. 191–192).

The question naturally arises, "If human beings are essentially soul and spirit, why must we undergo this darkened consciousness, these earthly struggles, and endure such pain? Why can't we remain highly conscious beings in the spiritual world?" It is the goal of Earth evolution to develop love. In order to love, we must experience freedom. A love compelled is no love at all. This freedom is experienced through our separation from the spiritual world in our physical bodies. But into this bodily constitution that separates us from spirit, the spirit, *with our cooperation*, can penetrate. We can elaborate our freedom through real thinking (page 111). Through thinking we can create a rational coherence to our lives. Through thinking we can transform feelings. Through thinking we can strengthen our will. "Nature subjects us to the laws of metabolism, but as human beings we subject ourselves to the laws of thought" (*Theosophy*, p. 30). We have the capacity to strengthen our thinking, deepening it to include the heart and the will, raising ourselves to higher levels of consciousness.

Every human being longs for the truth. Our search for the truth leads to wisdom, and only through wisdom can we attain love. "Beginning with the Earth phase of evolution, the wisdom of the outer cosmos becomes inner wisdom in the human being. Internalized in this way, it becomes the seed of love. Wisdom is the prerequisite for love; love is the result of wisdom that has been reborn in the I" (OES, p. 397). The I is unique. It is personal. It is separate. It can live in freedom.

Inner wisdom, the personal attainment of understanding, can be found only on Earth. Spiritual science

> cannot arise through the spiritual world as such. It arises only on Earth and can then be taken upward by human beings into the spiritual world.... Supersensible beings can only behold the supersensible world but cannot understand it. Concepts and ideas of the spiritual world can arise only on Earth, and they ray forth like a light into the spiritual world. This enables one to understand rightly the meaning of the Earth. The Earth is neither a mere transitional stage nor a vale of despair, but it exists so that on it a spiritual knowledge can be developed that can then be carried upward into the spiritual worlds (LBD&NB, pp. 307ff).

The ideas of spiritual science are not easy to comprehend. Steiner's books and lectures are intended to stimulate inner activity in us. This is particularly true of the exercises and meditations given in *How to Know Higher Worlds.* As soon as we *experience* this inner activity we experience ourselves as spirit. It is a sense-free experience. I *know* that it's not my brain spitting out thoughts as the liver produces bile. I know it is my innermost self, the attentiveness of my I-being, directing and utilizing the brain and sense organs to carry out my spiritual intentions. Through this experience we find our heart opening to the words communicated by an initiate describing higher worlds and deeper states of consciousness.

Steiner is not addressing the abstract human-being-in-general. He is speaking to me. He is speaking to you. Here in this particular place. At this particular time. Just as we have muscles and bones that anchor us to this physical, natural world, he would have us come alive in the spiritual world as we grasp the content of spiritual ideas and find our anchor in the world of spirit. We can do this only in a personal way, through our own decision, with our own inner activity.

It is just through plunging more deeply into the personal element that we inform ourselves not only how man-in-general, man-in-the-abstract has his roots in the spiritual world; we experience how every one of us, in our most personal aspect, in our experience as full individuals living in a particular time and place on Earth, is rooted in a wholly elementary way in a spiritual world to which he belongs and which bears the hallmark of eternity. And in his sensing of this he also has the feeling that a voice calls to him saying, "Don't make yourself into a soul-spiritual cripple with unhealthy spiritual content, for our reliance on you is not just a general one; it is a reliance on you to the extent that you are an entirely personal, individual human being" (PL II, p. 14).

Our experiences in the sense-world are not finished once we have the experience. Nor are they finished as our personal memory, "for while we experience things, while we form concepts, and feelings rise up in our experiences, the whole world of the hierarchies is active within this process through which we acquire experiences; the hierarchies live and weave in it" (LBD, p. 130). Imagine that when we are gazing at another person the hierarchies are living in our gaze, that we are looking with the eyes of the hierarchies; and that in the gaze of the other, the hierarchies gaze back at us. "In reality, the gods work within our experiences. We think that we live for our own sake; yet the gods work out something that they can weave into the world" (*ibid.,* p. 131). When we die, our life's experiences are given over to the cosmos, which gives the gods something to work with for the advancement of evolution. We feel this as the purpose of our lives. "The gods gave us the chance to live in order that they might spin out something for themselves, thus enriching the world…. This is an overwhelming thought. Every one of our strides is the external expression of an event connected with the gods…. Our human destinies are, at the same time, the deeds of gods" (*ibid.*).

*   *   *

We spoke of three basic concepts in anthroposophy that form the image of the human being: that we are composed of body, soul, and spirit; the laws of karma and reincarnation; and the capacity for self-transformation. These ideas are echoed in the Rosicrucian motto: *Ex Deo nascimur* (from God we are born); *In Christo morimur* (in Christ we die); *Per Spiritum Sanctum reviviscimus* (we are resurrected in the Holy Spirit). At the Christmas Foundation Conference Rudolf Steiner recast this motto as part of a Foundation Stone Mantra, which was set into the hearts of some

800 members attending: *From God, humankind has being; In Christ, death becomes life; In the Spirit's Universal Thoughts, the soul awakens.*[8]

* * *

The main sources for this introduction and appendix are from the following works of Rudolf Steiner:

Theosophy. Anthroposophic Press, Hudson, NY, 1993.

An Outline of Esoteric Science. Anthroposophic Press, Hudson, NY, 1997 (OES).

Life Between Death and New Birth. Rudolf Steiner Press, London, 1968 (LBD&NB) (Sixteen lectures throughout Europe, 1912-1913).

Life Beyond Death. Rudolf Steiner Press, London, 1995 (LBD).

The two public lectures given in The Hague: *Anthroposophy as a Need of the Age,* Nov. 15, 1923 (PL 1); and *Anthroposophy as a Human and Personal Way of Life,* Nov.16, 1923 (PL II), available in typescript under the title *The Transcendent Human Being.*

---

8. Zeylmans van Emmichoven, *The Foundation Stone*, Rudolf Steiner Press, London, 1963.

Further Reading

Essential Works by Rudolf Steiner

Anthroposophical Leading Thoughts. London: Rudolf Steiner Press, 1998.

How to Know Higher Worlds: A Modern Path of Initiation. Hudson, NY: Anthroposophic Press, 1994.

Intuitive Thinking as a Spiritual Path: A Philosophy of Freedom. Hudson, NY: Anthroposophic Press, 1994.

An Outline of Esoteric Science. Hudson, NY: Anthroposophic Press, 1998.

Theosophy: An Introduction to the Spiritual Processes in Human Life and in the Cosmos. Hudson, NY: Anthroposophic Press, 1994.

A Way of Self Knowledge: Meditation and the Soul's Path to Spiritual Experience (includes *The Threshold of the Spiritual World*). Hudson, NY: Anthroposophic Press, 1999.

Related Works by Rudolf Steiner

Angels: Selected Lectures by Rudolf Steiner. Anna Meuss (ed.). London: Rudolf Steiner Press, 1996.

Anthroposophy (A Fragment): A New Foundation for the Study of Human Nature. Hudson, NY: Anthroposophic Press, 1996.

Anthroposophy and the Inner Life. Bristol, UK: Rudolf Steiner Press, 1994.

At the Gates of Spiritual Science. London: Rudolf Steiner Press, 1986.

An Autobiography: Chapters in the Course of My Life, 1861–1907. Hudson, NY: Anthroposophic Press, 1999.

Between Death and Rebirth. London: Rudolf Steiner Press, 1975.

Christianity as Mystical Fact. Hudson, NY: Anthroposophic Press, 1997.

Cosmic and Human Metamorphoses. Blauvelt, NY: Garber Communications, 1989.

Cosmic Memory. Blauvelt, NY: Garber Communications, 1998.

The Destinies of Individuals and of Nations. London: Rudolf Steiner Press, 1986.

Earthly Death and Cosmic Life. London: Rudolf Steiner Press, 1964.

The Forming of Destiny & Life after Death. Blauvelt, New York: Garber Communications, 1989.

The Inner Nature of Man and the Life between Death and a New Birth. London: Rudolf Steiner Press, 1994.

Karmic Relationships: Esoteric Studies. 8 vols. London: Rudolf Steiner Press, 1972–1997.

Life between Death and Rebirth. Hudson, NY: Anthroposophic Press, 1989.

Life between Death and New Birth. London: Rudolf Steiner Press, 1968.

Life beyond Death. Frank Teichmann, (ed.). London: Rudolf Steiner Press, 1995.

Man's Being, His Destiny, and World Evolution. Hudson, NY: Anthroposophic Press, 1966.

The Presence of the Dead on the Spiritual Path. Hudson, NY: Anthroposophic Press, 1990.

A Psychology of Body, Soul & Spirit: Anthroposophy, Psychosophy, Pneumatosophy. Hudson, NY: Anthroposophic Press, 1999.

Spiritual Beings in the Heavenly Bodies and in the Kingdoms of Nature. Hudson, NY: Anthroposophic Press, 1992.

The Spiritual Guidance of the Individual and of Humanity. Hudson, NY: Anthroposophic Press, 1992.

The Spiritual Hierarchies and the Physical World: Reality and Illusion. Hudson, NY: Anthroposophic Press, 1996.

The Stages of Higher Knowledge. Hudson, NY: Anthroposophic Press, 1967.

Staying Connected: How to Continue Your Relationships with Those Who Have Died. C. Bamford (ed.). Hudson, NY: Anthroposophic Press, 1999.

Theosophy of the Rosicrucian. London: Rudolf Steiner Press, 1975.

A Western Approach to Reincarnation & Karma. René Querido (ed.). Hudson, NY: Anthroposophic Press, 1997.

Other Related Works

Archiati, Pietro. *Reincarnation in Modern Life: Towards a New Christian Awareness.* London: Temple Lodge Publishing, 1998.

Barnes, Henry. *A Life for the Spirit: Rudolf Steiner in the Crosscurrents of Our Time.* Hudson, NY: Anthroposophic Press, 1997.

McDermott, Robert (ed.), *The Essential Steiner.* San Francisco: Harper-SanFrancisco, 1984.

Roszell, Calvert. *The Near-Death Experience: In the Light of Scientific Research and the Spiritual Science of Rudolf Steiner.* Hudson, NY: Anthroposophic Press, 1992.

During the last two decades of the nineteenth century, the Austrian-born Rudolf Steiner (1861–1925) became a respected and well-published scientific, literary, and philosophical scholar, particularly known for his work on Goethe's scientific writings. After the turn of the century he began to develop his earlier philosophical principles into an approach to methodical research of psychological and spiritual phenomena.

His multifaceted genius has led to innovative and holistic approaches in medicine, philosophy, religion, education (Waldorf schools), special education, economics, science, agriculture (Biodynamic method), architecture, drama, the new arts of speech and eurythmy, and other fields of activity. In 1924 he founded the General Anthroposophical Society, which today has branches throughout the world.